SITUATIONAL
MANAGEMENT
a contingency approach to leadership

SITUATIONAL MANAGEMENT

a contingency approach to leadership

HOWARD M. CARLISLE

a division of American Management Associations

International standard book number: 0-8144-5330-9
Library of Congress catalog card number: 73-79242

First printing

to my wife, Colleen

preface

IN THIS BOOK I present a new methodology called situational analysis, and my reasons for doing so include some personal history. After World War II, I took a bachelor's degree, spent three years in graduate school, and then worked in various administrative capacities for ten years. My experience was about evenly split between business and government. In 1963 I became a professor of management. I have thoroughly enjoyed teaching, but I have never felt quite comfortable with the approach to management I find in current textbooks and most of the literature. It never quite fits my experiences as an administrator. All too often, management literature seems too nebulous, too generalized, and too compartmentalized to be as meaningful as it should be for the practitioner. Viewing management as functions, processes, and broad principles is useful, but it fails to provide the orientation and the realistic framework I think necessary on the basis of my own experience.

Accordingly, I have been searching for a means of presenting management knowledge and practice that would more nearly coincide with the experiences of managers. My first findings were reported in an article entitled "Measuring the Situational Nature of Management" (*California Management Review*, Winter 1968 issue). In brief, I had become convinced that different managers in different organizations face different situations that require different solutions. Those differences point up the need for an approach to management that includes an analysis of differences and an interpretation of their meaning for management theory and practice.

Recent developments in management theory have been moving in the same direction. Insights provided by systems theory, the contributions from the behavioral and quantitative sciences, and the reaction of traditional management theory to those influences have opened the way for the situational approach. Management in the 1960s was on the verge of a major shift from its traditional base. The mood of the period was to recognize the inadequacies and see the conflict and lack of integration in existing theory and practice.

Thus, the way has been opened for a new synthesis and novel approaches. My own effort is to present a general text on management that is based on situational analysis. It represents a rather sharp departure from the traditional view of planning, organizing, leading, controlling, decision making, and the other responsibilities of a manager. The analytical methodology involved is in many respects more detailed and yet more comprehensive than that normally undertaken in the past. Hopefully, the book presents a management theory that will be more relevant and useful to the practicing manager. Certainly, however, it is no panacea. Its concepts offer considerable potential as a new basis for management thought; but because they are still in the developmental stage, they lack broad empirical support. They will require a long period of practical application, research documentation, and discussion before they can be highly useful. In many respects this book offers some first approximations for further investigations.

Like any other author, I am indebted to many people, far too many to enumerate here. I am especially grateful to the writers who applied systems theory to the field of management and provided many insights that are contained in this book. I would also like to express appreciation to Dr. Krishna Shetty, my colleague at Utah State University, who has spent many hours discussing these concepts with me. Finally, I am indebted to my wife, Colleen, and to my children—Richard, Julie, Jana Lou, and Michael—who have been tolerant and understanding through the entire span of this writing project.

Howard M. Carlisle

contents

Contents

one
the situational nature of management

GARY ROBERTSON was a senior chemist employed by a major industrial firm located in the eastern part of the United States. His career pattern was fairly typical for someone in his profession. He attended college for eight years, received a doctorate in chemistry, and then for the next twelve years was employed by the same firm as a research chemist. Over the twelve years he was given progressively more responsibility and assigned to more difficult projects, but essentially his total effort was directed at research. Then the director of the laboratory unexpectedly decided to retire and the company asked Gary to take his place.

Gary was decidedly taken aback, but after a week of wrestling with the question, he decided to accept. The reason for his reluctance was not self-doubt; it was simply that all his training and experience were related to the technical aspects of chemical research. He did not have the background for administering a laboratory that employed 350 people and had a budget of $8 million. He knew he would be thoroughly comfortable with the technical decisions he would have to face; it was the administrative ones that gave him pause. But that, he felt, was only because they were unfamiliar. He had two months to prepare for his new position, and so he did what any well-trained scientist would do: he went to the literature on management, supervision, and leadership.

He was astonished by the vast amount of information on what he thought were relatively uncomplicated subjects. The local university library had, not a dozen or so, but hundreds of books on management. He was just as staggered by the periodicals—he had expected perhaps half a dozen and found over a hundred listed in the business and management serials catalog. There were mountains of information on general management, on all of the specific processes of management, on all of the functional areas of management, and on the thousands of techniques with which a manager should, presumably, be at least familiar.

Gary saw at once that he would be overwhelmed by the material if he were not selective, so he next went to his company's training director for help. The director was both sympathetic and cooperative; he loaned Gary some "good introductory books" on general management. But once again, Gary had found no easy solution. All the books were divided into sections in which such major subjects as planning, organizing, leading, and controlling were considered. Each section included a discussion of the principles that were related to the process, and the principles were advanced as being universal. They were universal because they could be applied by all managers in all types of organizations, business or otherwise.

The trouble was that Gary could not relate the so-called universal principles to the research laboratory he was going to administer. Some were so general and vague as to be either valueless or self-evident; others

2

seemed to be appropriate for an assembly process but not an R&D laboratory. He was quite sure that many of them would be viewed with alarm and skepticism by his research colleagues. A few did appear to be of potential benefit to him as a laboratory administrator, but too often he was frustrated when he tried to think through their specific applicability to his future position.

Gary also reviewed many of the recent issues of the more popular management journals. He found them full of articles on a wide range of topics in both the behavioral and the quantitative sciences. Occasionally he found an article that had application to his situation as he saw it, but more often than not he found none. After a good deal of searching, he did find some literature that dealt specifically with the management of R&D laboratories, but even that failed him because the problems and circumstances were unique.

What troubled Gary most was the lack of what he considered to be a valid framework for dealing with the responsibilities of supervision. He was still uncertain about the specific skills and knowledge an effective executive must have. He was still struggling with the concept of management; he was skeptical of the validity of the broad generalities used to describe the management process and divide it into subfields. In particular, the universalist approach just did not make sense. He strongly suspected that the knowledge and skills that he would need in his new position as director of the laboratory were different from those he had needed to head up a research task force; he was absolutely certain they were quite different from those required by a controller or purchasing agent. The positions might involve similar administrative responsibilities, but each was unique in regard to the decisions that must be made, the problems that must be faced, and the resources that must be utilized.

Gary's problem was not, of course, unique. Many aspiring and practicing administrators experience difficulty in relating the alleged concepts, principles, and techniques of management to their individual circumstances. Consequently, questions about the relevance of those concepts, principles, and techniques are frequently raised. Many are those in search of a theory that adequately encompasses what they are doing or hope to do, and many are those who search in vain. The current offerings frequently seem to be too broad, too simplistic, and too devoid of meaning.

Research studies in management have the same shortcomings. Major efforts have been directed at determining whether the people-oriented supervisor is more effective than the production- or task-oriented one, as if that were the only major variable in productivity. New organization concepts or planning principles are espoused without an adequate effort to identify the situations in which they are most appropriate. Quantitative methods are offered with no warning of the limits within which they are useful. Principles that actually apply to only one situation are advanced as general management knowledge on the basis of the universalist assumption.

MANAGEMENT AS A STUDY

The current status of management thought and practice can best be appreciated by reviewing the events that led to the present predicament. A study of the behavior of people in groups is almost as old as history, but management as a concrete body of knowledge with some scientific underpinnings is less than a century old. Frederick Taylor, who lived from 1856 to 1917, and is generally considered to have inaugurated that study, did most of his significant research, inquiry, and writing in the twentieth century.

Taylor was a highly successful engineer in the United States iron and steel industry. He observed the way in which work was performed in the shops and work areas and was impressed by the haphazard, inconsistent sequence of the methods used. He became convinced that there was one best way to perform any given physical task and that it could be discovered by careful analysis and investigation. After observation of and controlled experimentation with laborers performing physical work, he derived what he considered to be the optimal motions, methods, and sequencing of tasks to maximize efficiency. His emphasis on a precise, analytical approach became known as "scientific management." His legacy was more than his emphasis on a methodical approach to the analysis of shop methods; it was also his belief in the "one best way" to perform tasks, organize work, and manage operations.

Fayol's Contribution

Henri Fayol, a French contemporary of Taylor, was also highly successful in his country's iron and steel industry. He is frequently called the father of modern management because he provided the framework that has dominated management thought since his time. He was careful to distinguish between technical and managerial skills. The latter, he said, were distinct from the traditional finance, production, and distribution functions. Management skills consist of planning, organizing, commanding, coordinating, and controlling.

Since Fayol's time management has been circumscribed and dissected into subfields based upon his "process approach." Indeed, the process structure has dominated the development of management theory and knowledge; it has provided the most commonly used framework for explaining the activities involved in supervision and describing the scope and content of managerial responsibility. Fayol did not single-handedly develop this approach to management; similar developments were under way in the United States and other English-speaking countries. In fact, Fayol's works were not widely published in English until the 1940s. He did, however, provide a more comprehensive and better integrated framework than most of his contemporaries.

Fayol, like Taylor, wanted to develop principles on which the best managerial decisions could be based. He developed 14 of them—a partial list of "acknowledged truths regarded as proven on which to rely." [1] According to Fayol, these were truths that all managers in all organizations should know, because they represented the best way to organize, plan, command, coordinate, and control the activities of subordinates. Among them were the now-familiar principles of unity of command, unity of direction, the scalar chain, an emphasis on centralization and specialization, and a strong plea for order ("a place for everyone and everyone in his place").

Again like Taylor, Fayol wanted to discover the one best way. Like most other writers, however, he was very cautious in regard to managerial activities; he acknowledged that "there is nothing rigid or absolute in management affairs" and that "principles are flexible and capable of adaptation to every need." [2] However, as is true of most themes that come to dominate social movements, the floodwater of change washed away the qualifications made and the limits set by the original advocate.

Developments Following Fayol

In the early years of management literature, the writers struggled to gain respect for their discipline. As had been demonstrated in the sciences, respect could be achieved only through the development of a body of knowledge and principles that could be used for predictive purposes. In their rush to transform management from an art to a science, the writers relied on the themes of Fayol and Taylor. The management texts that began to appear in the 1940s and 1950s were patterned after Fayol's principles approach; in 1945 Alvin Brown elaborated 96 principles of organization. The search for principles of general validity for all managers in all types of organizations dominated the first 70 years of the systematic development of management theory and knowledge.

The Universalist Tradition

In the 1960s it became more common for management practitioners, researchers, and writers to challenge the assumptions underlying the classical approaches. Neither the validity nor the importance of the earlier contributions was denied; what was challenged was the extension of

5

those contributions, the direction in which classical thought would ultimately lead. It went without saying that Taylor, Fayol, and others were largely responsible for the rapid advance in management theory and practice; without their emphasis on method, management science would certainly be at a more primitive stage of development. Progress in both theory and practice has probably been as rapid as it could have been with any other theoretical structure.

THE SITUATIONALIST VIEWPOINT

The era of traditional management theory has provided, in a scientific methodology and sound concepts, a foundation from which a step forward in the development of management theory can be made. The need for change became evident in the 1960s, when both practitioners and writers discovered the difficulties with which Gary Robertson was confronted when he looked for help in preparing himself for his new position. The solid foundation of concepts and techniques * had resulted from the flood of research and conceptual applications after World War II; some experts estimate that 90 percent of management knowledge has been developed since 1945. With so much to choose from, the manager's problem has become that of discovering in which situations and under what circumstances a particular set of concepts or techniques will work best. These are not principles that can be applied across the board; they are principles that must be selected according to the particular problem or situation at hand. Just as a doctor, even in this day of miracle drugs, has no universal remedy but must first find out what is wrong with the patient, so the manager must select the tools and concepts that are appropriate to his particular situation.

The supervision problem, then, is twofold: knowing the concepts, principles, and techniques that are available to the manager and being able to analyze the particular situation as a basis for determining which of the available concepts, principles, and techniques will be most effective in that situation. That represents a sharp contrast to traditional theory and practice. The emphasis has been on the similarities of organizations and circumstances; the search has been for the best way of managing one organization so it can be applied to all organizations. In contrast, the situational approach postulates a managerial decision that is contingent on the circumstances. Thus the emphasis is placed on knowing how management situations differ and how those differences will affect the applica-

---

* In this book, the terms "concepts" and "techniques" are used interchangeably, although it is recognized that concepts are abstract ideas or generalizations that enhance understanding, and techniques are specific methods for accomplishing a desired result.

tion of management knowledge. Instead of trying to identify the similarities in organizations, the effort is to identify the dissimilarities and interpret what they will mean in management practice.

Above all, the situationalist holds that there is no one best way to manage. Taylor may have been right when he said there is one best way to perform a repetitive physical task, but that is not true of planning, organizing, leading, controlling, or decision making. Different organizations with different tasks and different competitive environments require different plans. No one would expect a social club, a giant corporation, and a small family business to be organized in the same way. In each the leadership style must be related to the personality of the leader and the skill, training, and attitudes of the followers. Just as every human personality and every organization is unique, so every managerial position or situation is unique.

This entire book is based upon the major premise that there is no one best way to handle any of the various management functions. There is no one best way to plan; there is no one best way to lead; there is no one best way to organize a group; and there is no one best way to control the activities of an organization. The best concepts and techniques can be selected only after one is aware of the particular circumstances he is facing. Even that statement is open to challenge. There are those who advance the equifinality concept: an equally effective solution to any given problem can be reached by any one of several means. According to that viewpoint, there are many effective means of solving a management problem and also many ineffective ones; the manager must select one of the former and avoid all of the latter. If it were possible to identify the top twelve organization experts in the United States and then get their opinion on how to solve a particular organizational problem, the likely result would be twelve different answers. All the approaches would be effective and perhaps even similar, but each would be likely to have some variations. To get the experts to concur on the one best way would probably be impossible.

The theoretical structure of management knowledge has been developed with the one-best-way assumption as a major tenet. Thus the current problem is to revise, reconstruct, or redirect existing theory so that it can serve as a springboard for the next phase of development. Until then, management theory will continue its erratic course and practitioners will continue to question its relevance. In the balance of this book an attempt is made to weave a situational fabric that holds promise of being the beginning of such a reconstructed theory. That theory will be the basis for thoroughly pragmatic management practice.

two
situational differences

THE BEST WAY to appreciate situational analysis is to explore in detail the factors that constitute the primary differences in various situations. If we can identify those factors, we can then determine how they affect the application of management concepts and techniques. To that end, an example more detailed than the one of the preceding chapter will be presented. In it two different management situations will be contrasted; one involves an engineering activity and the other a production activity.

TWO MANAGEMENT SITUATIONS

Frank Rogers is employed by an aerospace firm that has 30,000 workers engaged in the research, development, and production phases of five different major aerospace programs. He is a supervisor of a department that handles all the engineering for a missile system that is one of the five programs. In Frank's department there are 75 professional engineers divided into six sections that deal with separate aspects of missile design —case, propellant, nozzle, and so on. The entire missile system requires an extension of the current state of the art; that is, the engineers are attempting to come up with advanced designs that will give the missile performance characteristics superior to those of present operational missiles.

The tasks involved in Frank's department are experimental, sophisticated, and unstructured. Each section is engaged in highly specialized research the details of which are familiar only to the experts who constitute the workforce in that section. For that reason the current status of the work is very difficult to communicate to cost accountants, marketing representatives, and even general managers. Moreover, the unpredictability of the work makes difficult any forecast of progress in relation to either time or resources required. In sum, the ordinary systems by which output or performance is monitored, measured, and controlled lack standards or benchmarks established by prior experience. Also, the absence of any physical output that can be counted or otherwise measured makes the evaluation of performance very difficult.

Darrell Hendricks is a shift supervisor in the cutting section of a food-processing plant. The plant, which is located in an agricultural community, was established primarily to process potatoes into frozen food products such as french fries. Now corn and beans are processed prior to the potato season. The work force is 200 employees year-round and builds up to over 1,000 at the potato harvest. Most of the seasonal employees are women from the community who assist in the various potato-processing operations. The potatoes are first immersed in a caustic solution that dissolves most of the peel; after that they are moved by conveyers to the cutting section.

On his shift Darrell supervises 80 women who cut the eyes and blemishes out of the potatoes. All 80 perform the same job. The work is routine and repetitive, and it requires little skill other than physical dexterity. As a result, no formal training program is required and the wage rates are relatively low. The production output of each shift is carefully measured and compared with that of other shifts and with the figures from other years. Supervisors are frequently rotated on a shift basis, and that causes little disruption because they are familiar with all the processing operations. Among the hourly employees turnover and absenteeism tend to be quite high. The employees are unionized and grievances are relatively common, although strikes are infrequent.

SIMILARITIES IN THE SITUATIONS

In many respects Frank and Darrell have similar but in other respects different activities and responsibilities. Both have the responsibility of attempting to achieve the goals or results that are desired—perhaps even demanded—by their organizations; both have the responsibility of effectively and efficiently utilizing company resources to achieve those goals or results; both have the responsibility of leading the employees in their work groups in a manner that will maximize productivity.

In doing all that they engage in many common management processes. They are responsible in varying degrees for planning and scheduling activities within their work groups; they assign and reassign people to different work locations or different tasks; they typically have some say over the selection of people who are employed in their organizations; they listen to the complaints of subordinates and encourage, reprimand, or take other action they feel is necessary; they monitor and control the work performed; they communicate the status of their activities to higher-level managers both verbally and in writing; and they make a variety of other decisions that affect the functioning of their work groups. Those activities are, of course, only a few examples of the many that commonly typify supervisory practice.

DIFFERENCES IN THE SITUATIONS

Although the activities of the two supervisors are similar as to type, they are dissimilar as to specifics and the supervisory actions required. Essentially, every aspect of the environments that the two managers face is characterized by major differences. The problems involved, the job factors that are dominant and need attention, and the ingredients of success are different. Because of the situational differences, the concepts, techniques, and management systems the supervisor applies and works with will fre-

11

quently be different. That both managers are engaged in planning, organizing, leading, controlling, and decision making does not mean that the concepts and techniques they select and apply in those activities are the same. Different concepts and techniques will be successful in different situations; the demands of the situation dictate the choice of concepts and techniques to be applied.

Some of the primary situational differences to be expected in the aerospace and food-processing examples are considered here. The differences are grouped by the factors that are most significant in management activities. In these comparisons the other-things-being-equal assumption applies. In management practice, however, rarely are other things equal. Therefore, even though these conditions are likely, they will obviously not hold for all aerospace and food-processing firms. That becomes even more evident with the recognition that it is not only the different states of the factors themselves but also their interrelations that create the composite situation.

Overall Differences in Business Operations

• The critical function—the dominant issue in terms of success—would likely be production for the processing plant and research and development for the aerospace firm. The result would be emphasis on efficiency and cost control in one firm and on technical capability in the other.

• Production in the processing plant would be a high-volume, short-cycle and single, repetitive process; in the aerospace firm it would be a low-volume, long-cycle, and multiprocess involving the assembly of thousands of parts.

• Because of the totally different products and markets, the pricing policies, channels of distribution, and methods of promotion would all likely be different for the two firms.

• Labor relations would differ because one group is unionized and the other is not.

Differences in People, Tasks, and Technology

• The training, educational background, and skill level of the two groups of employees would differ.

• Activities in the cutting section involve essentially physical skills; those in engineering, mental ones.

• Attitudes and job-oriented norms of the employees would differ consistent with the respective professional and nonprofessional backgrounds of engineers and food processors.

• Of the two groups, the engineers would be more likely to be highly identified with their tasks, and that would also affect their commitment to their employer.

• In respect to employee needs, expectations, and aspirations, each group would be relatively homogeneous but the two groups would be very different.

• The man–machine interface would be more complex in the potato-processing operations, in which machinery is extensively involved, than in engineering, with its limited use of machinery.

• There would likely be more pressures for conformity in the cutting operations and more outlets for creativity and innovation in the engineering activities.

• The cutting operations, which involve routine, repetitive tasks, normally would not offer any intrinsic challenge or reward.

• Because the salaries offered and the backgrounds required for the positions would differ, the management experience and knowledge of the two supervisors would also differ.

• Technical engineering activities directed at advancing the state of the art would be much less predictable than the more routine production operations.

Differences in Structure and Organization

• The major subdivisions of the firms would be organized on a process basis in the potato plant and on a program or product basis in the aerospace plant.

• The larger, more complex aerospace firm would have more levels in its organizational hierarchy.

• The span of control—the number of subordinates reporting to a supervisor—would be higher in the routine, single-task, food-processing operations than in the more complex engineering activities.

• In the smaller firm, with its less complex tasks, there would likely be more centralization of authority at the top of the organization.

• In the larger firm, with its more complex tasks and greater resources, there would be more special staff services to assist the line supervisors.

• In the more dynamic environment of the aerospace firm there would be more frequent changes in the organization structure and greater use of temporary groups such as task forces and committees.

• The personal roles and informal groups in the two companies would differ because the backgrounds, needs, interests, and objectives of the two groups of employees are different.

• Because of the pressures for conformity and the lack of psychological appeal in the production tasks, a more autocratic approach to supervision could be expected of the cutting section supervisors.

• Because of the technical nature of engineering activities and the un-

predictability of specific engineering tasks, decision making would be more complex in the aerospace plant.
• Decision making in the aerospace engineering department would probably focus on technical problems; in the more routine food-processing operations it would likely focus on people problems.
• The authority of the lower-level supervisor would be restricted in the centralized processing plant, but the lack of support and staff services would likely make his range of responsibilities greater.
• Because the aerospace firm is working under government contract, major decisions on design, cost, and schedule would be participated in or even made exclusively by the government.

Differences in Planning and Control Concepts and Systems

• The more routine potato-processing operations would foster planning and control systems associated with flow control and quality; the innovative aerospace operations would foster planning and control systems associated with one-of-a-kind projects and thus involve a network analysis approach such as the program evaluation and review technique (PERT) or a Gantt-chart approach such as milestone scheduling.
• Historical cost and production standards in the food-processing plant would make planning and control more specific, detailed, and predictable than in the aerospace plant.
• By the nature of its operations and the data available, the food-processing plant would have a process cost system and a flexible-type budget, whereas the aerospace plant would have a job order cost system and a fixed-type budget.
• The highly technical, diverse activities of the aerospace plant would foster more complex planning and control systems. The same complexity would make management information systems and other forms of communication more complex also.
• The many diverse operations would make coordination a greater problem in the aerospace plant than in the food-processing plant.

Differences in Broad Environmental Considerations

• Advancing technology would have a much greater impact on the aerospace firm because of the high technological content of its operations.
• Although governmental and political considerations would affect both organizations, they would have a greater effect on the aerospace firm because of its primary dependence on government contracts.
• The greater size of the aerospace firm would increase the possibility of its affecting environmental forces rather than merely reacting to them.
• The economic markets of the two firms would vary significantly in

number and size of buyers and sellers, the amount of product differentiation, and other ways that affect the constraints a manager must work within and the decisions he must make.

THE NATURE AND CHALLENGES OF MANAGEMENT

The comparison of the two firms supports several significant conclusions regarding the basic management processes:

First, it reaffirms that there is no one best method of organizing group activity. Organizational methods must be based on such factors as the task to be performed and the nature of the skills, knowledge, and capability of the people required to perform those tasks.

Second, it supports the conclusion that there is no universal method or system for planning and controlling the activities of an organization. The nature of the tasks performed and the predictability of their outcome are two of the key factors that dictate the utilization of specific planning and control concepts.

Third, and perhaps most important, situational conclusions of the same kind can be made regarding leadership. No one leadership style is universally applicable and invariably superior to other approaches to supervision. The effectiveness of leadership styles depends on the factors present in the situation. The situational factors and their interrelationship generate conditions conducive to specific types of leadership. The work situation factors that most affect leadership styles tend to be the tasks performed, the technological complexity of the tasks, the training, background, attitudes, and needs of the workers, the organizational climate, and the time constraints placed on the organization.

These three conclusions constitute a realistic appraisal of the nature and challenges of management. It is true that managers are engaged in the common processes of decision making, planning, organizing, leading, and controlling, but broad, universal generalizations must almost stop there. The task of the manager is to select from the many concepts, techniques, and management systems available those that will be effective in his particular situation. As the situation is changed by either internal or external pressures, the manager must be flexible enough to adjust his methods, concepts, and systems. As a program progresses from R&D into production, for example, he must adjust his planning and control systems. As engineers are phased out and production workers are phased in, supervisors with different training and leadership styles will likely be appropriate.

The Contingency Approach

A premise of the contingency approach to management is that one of the key skills of a supervisor is the ability to size up a situation. The supervisory challenge is to evaluate factors such as the resource mix needed to conduct operations, complexity of tasks, the appeal that certain tasks have for worker-need satisfaction, employee attitudes, the social forces at work in an organization, the power structure of the organization, the expectations of higher-level management, and so forth. Based on his ability to evaluate such key factors, the supervisor then selects courses of action, adopts planning and control systems, and makes other key decisions that will be effective given the situational constraints. The great need, again, is for a theoretical framework to assist the manager in doing all this.

three
the contingency model of management

THIS CHAPTER PROVIDES a contingency model of management based on situational analysis. It is proposed as an evolutionary advance over the functional-principles model that has been predominantly used in the development of traditional management. The model having been presented, the balance of the book will be devoted to further examination of the primary factors, applications of the model, and, particularly, the management practice implications. First, however, the rationale for developing the model must be made clear. The model should meet these requirements:

1. *It should serve as a framework in which to collect, assess, and further develop management knowledge.* Any specific bit of information is of limited value until it can be related to and combined with other information. When information can be classified and integrated in that fashion, it leads to the development of postulates, hypotheses, and principles; those principles in turn generate more knowledge and information.

2. *It should provide more understanding of the basic nature of the management process.* It should focus on many factors, not just one or two, and so be much more realistic to the practitioner. The focus is more meaningful because it tends to highlight interrelationships and interdependencies among the factors. The emphasis on cause-and-effect relationships should be a major advance over the primarily descriptive approaches used in the past.

3. *It should provide better tools for measuring management knowledge.* Much of the vagueness of management thought arises from a primary reliance on terminology that is in ordinary use and is not restricted to one discipline. Typical management terminology is rife with multiple meanings, loose connotations, and confusing overlaps. Management can advance as a science only when better communication and measurement tools are developed. To avoid the problem of semantics, management theory must ultimately rely more heavily on information that can be quantified. One of the primary features of the contingency model proposal is a set of scales for measuring or evaluating the primary variables that dominate management situations.

4. *It should serve as a guide to management action.* Unless its primary advantage is ultimately to the practitioner, the model can have little real value. It should aid the manager in mapping situations and in understanding the forces that are at work in any particular situation. Once in hand, that understanding should provide a reliable guide to the selection and application of the various systems, methods, and techniques comprising the manager's bag of tools.

QUALIFICATIONS

As a necessary preliminary to the explanation of the model, a word of caution: At this stage in the development of the model, the primary interest is in the concept as a whole rather than a detailed examination and verification of each element. The strengths and weaknesses of the model will become more obvious with experience in its use. As further knowledge is developed, many changes and refinements will be necessary. In sum, the purpose of this book is to explain the model rather than to attempt to defend each of its features. Most of the major assumptions regarding the primary factors and their interrelationships are in fact supported by the findings of past research, but many of the details are provisional and need verification through future research activity. That, however, should not stand in the way of experimentation with and testing of the model by practitioners in their own management environments.

One further qualification is necessary. Even though the contingency model is much more comprehensive than most preceding models have been, no claim is made that all factors are included. Many of the dimensions presented are only suggestive of others that might be developed. The basic framework is mandatory and inviolate, that is, but many of the detailed attributes and dimensions are only suggestive of those that might be developed to add body to the basic structure.

FACTORS INTERNAL TO THE ORGANIZATION

The basic premise of the contingency approach is that the manager's primary task is to make decisions, select concepts, and behave in a way that will be effective in a particular situation. However, in any management situation or environment there are hundreds of interrelated factors, and the critical question for the manager is which of those factors are dominant or primary in their effect on the overall outcome and in modifying other factors. If a manager were required to evaluate all the factors in a situation, his task would be impossible. But if he can focus on a relatively few factors, not only is his job more feasible but generalizations on the more limited basis can be used as guides in his managerial activities.

Management practice and research point to five factors internal to the organization as the primary ones with which a manager must contend:

The *purpose* of the organization.
The *tasks* involved in the functioning of the organization.
The scientific content or *technology* of the tasks.
The *people* who perform the tasks.
The *structure* of the organization.

19

These factors are shown schematically in Figure 1. A manager is concerned with three aspects of the five factors: their intensity, their particular characteristics (hereafter also referred to as dimensions), and their interrelationship. Once a manager has assessed the factors by evaluating their dimensions, he has identified the primary ones internal to his organization, the ones on which his effectiveness in decision making and in the application of management methods and techniques depend. However, his diagnosis is not complete until he thoroughly understands the cause-and-effect relations of the factors.

The Purpose Factor

Basic to any organization is its fundamental purpose. Beyond it but inextricably related to it are the specific objectives of the participants and leaders in the organization. The purpose of the organization has a determining effect on the tasks, technology, people, and structure of the organization.

For example, if two individuals decide to earn their living by joining in partnership to establish a job shop in which they will perform a variety of machining operations, their purpose limits their other alternatives. Specifically, their purpose has restricted their choice in regard to the

Figure 1. **Factors internal to the organization.**

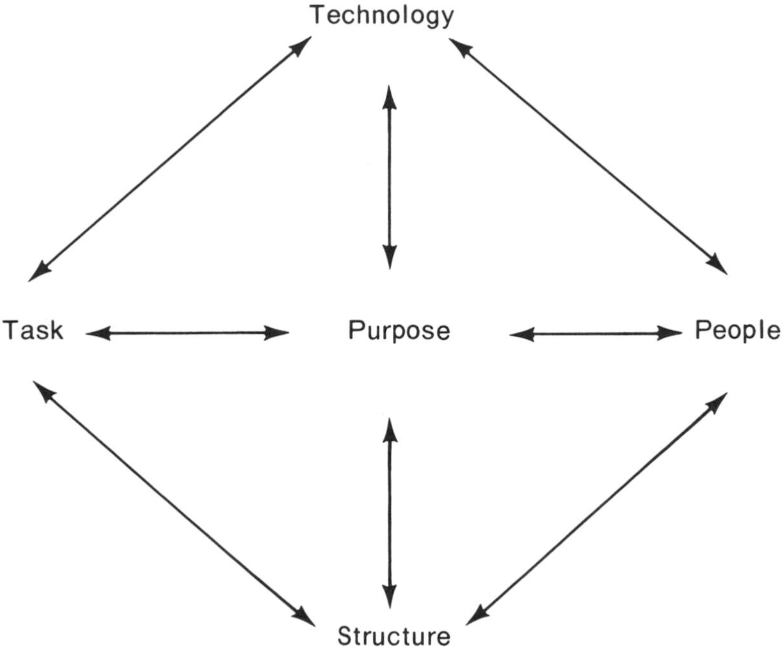

task, technology, and people factors. Given the stated purpose of the enterprise, machining operations will constitute the primary tasks to be performed. The technology of the tasks is associated with both the machine tools to be utilized and the machining operations involved. The people factor naturally follows the same pattern; individuals with training and experience in the various machining operations will be needed. The organization the partners establish will be structured in accordance with their decision to function as a job shop and engage in machining operations. The primary role of purpose in structuring the activities of an organization is reflected in Figure 1—the other four factors both surround and derive from the purpose.

Evaluating the purpose of a firm is not as easy as it might seem. If firms existed solely to make a profit and if providing goods or services were simply the means of making that profit, then the evaluation of purpose would be quite simple. However, all organizations have plural objectives, and not even the purpose of an industrial firm can be simply stated as profit maximization. That every organization has a variety of purposes is evident when immediate and intermediate objectives are considered and the separate personal goals of the individual participants are included.

People identify with an organization for reasons that are related to their needs. Obviously, their employment provides the income that they use for sustenance and for the other physical needs they satisfy in their outside activities. In addition, however, their employment provides them an opportunity to apply their skills and training. It can also reward them with social contacts and with the recognition given them for their performance. In that way institutional purpose and individual purpose become entangled in a complexity of human wants, desires, and expectations and the broader goals and needs of the organization.

An analysis of intermediate goals is rewarding for reason of the management insight it can provide. In the job shop example two individuals form a partnership for the purpose of making a living—an oversimplification that is acceptable for illustrative purposes. Their means of doing so is to establish a machine shop in which they will specialize in custom machining jobs. However, they have a variety of intermediate goals that relate to being effective in satisfying the needs of their customers. Typically those goals would include work of high quality on a timely basis at a reasonable cost. The intermediate objectives are the ones that have a dependent relation with certain dimensions of the task, technology, people, and structure factors. The intermediate objectives determine the machining processes, services to be offered, people employed, and other subfactors.

In a broader context it should be remembered that organizations exist in our society for a variety of purposes. In addition to organizations whose goals are basically economic, there are many others whose purposes are social, ethical, political, operational, or recreational. A few of the possibilities are suggested in Table 1.

The Task Factor

Tasks are the activities performed by the people who belong to an organization. The activities of machines are more properly referred to as machine operations or processes rather than tasks. On the other hand, the task factor covers the activities of both men and machines, although the focus is on the people-performed tasks. Tasks include the activities people are assigned to perform and also those they assume in achieving the goals and objectives of the organization. Production tasks consist of the activities performed in modifying an object either with or without the aid of machinery. Marketing tasks involve such activities as the selling efforts necessary to attract customers. Traditionally, that is, tasks have been defined on a functional basis and grouped into such categories as marketing, production, engineering, research, maintenance, and finance.

In addition to the skill specialization involved, there are other task dimensions that are of significance to the manager. The complexity of the task is extremely important; it depends on the degree to which tasks

Table 1. Analysis of organizational purpose.

Dimensions	*Means of Classification and Evaluation*
Basic purpose	Traditional measures such as profit, service, socialization, education, recreation, health care, and environmental improvement.
Economic goals	Traditional measures such as profit, return on investment, and price-earnings ratio.
Social goals	Provide particular services; attain specific need satisfaction; contribute to welfare of groups or individuals; etc.
Operational goals	Achieve certain production levels; accomplish specific projects; etc.
Utility goals	Descriptive measures of benefits desired, efficiencies achieved, or satisfaction provided.
Ethical goals	Attainment of specific standards or achievement of specific behavior.
Political goals	Power, control, modification of political institutions, etc.
Ownership	Public, private, governmental, foundation, or other.

involve working with people, things, and information. If the skills demanded are relatively simple and involve little knowledge or training, this situation has many implications in regard to the availability of people and the training they require, the nature of the supervision needed, and the planning, controlling, and reporting of the activities. The socio-technical considerations of interfacing tasks and machine operation also contribute to complexity. The nature of the tasks and machine operations are major determinants in decisions on resource allocation that are consistent with the basic input or output model of economics. In general, the more complex the tasks, the more complex the management required.

Other significant task dimensions are physical versus mental demands, the degree of repetition, the sequential interdependence of a series of tasks, the time range or job cycle, and the throughput rate or rate of flow of the operations. Those dimensions influence the demands of the task on the worker and hence the monotony of the task. They in turn affect behavior and motivation.

The dimensions that are important in defining the characteristics of the task factor are discussed in detail in Chapter 6. There it will be noted that most of them are to be evaluated by means of a scale that in some instances can be used to compare tasks. Conceiving tasks as continuums is more realistic than conceiving them to be some kind of absolutes. The dimensions of variables will frequently be related to a scale; they are based not on the assumption that all dimensions can be precisely measured but on the premise that all dimensions are relative to each other and to particular situations. Each of two tasks might be repetitive, but one task much more than the other—an assembler applying a torque wrench 25,000 times a day versus a sales clerk recording 100 sales in a day. The list of common dimensions given in Chapter 6 is not meant to be exhaustive; it is only representative of the primary characteristics of the task factor that are frequently significant in business operations.

The intensity and significance of the task in relation to other factors are determined by the dimensions that characterize that task. Simple, routine tasks provide little psychological need satisfaction to most workers. Tasks associated with assembly line operations involve close sequential interdependence and coordination that reduces the independence of the worker by forcing him to accomplish his tasks in an ordered, time-oriented pattern. Such situations frequently result in the need for a more structured, autocratic approach to supervision. Also, in such a situation management can expect minimal identification with either the task and/or the organization. That in turn invites morale problems and identification with secondary groups such as labor unions. The manner in which tasks are designated and structured has a direct deterministic influence on the functioning of the organization and on other key factors, especially people and technology.

The Technology Factor

Many writers and researchers, especially sociologists and anthropologists, do not differentiate between the task and technology factors. They consider technology to be a task characteristic that represents the complexity of the knowledge used in the work flow. However, if technology is designated as a characteristic of the task, it is easy to lose sight of the strong dependent relation that technology has with other factors and especially its bearing on the applicability and effectiveness of planning and control systems. Many managerial decisions are conditioned by the nature and status of technology in the organization.

Technology involves the mechanical or technical substance of a task or series of tasks. It consists of tools, techniques, processes, and knowledge that extend human capability. Complex engineering tasks involve high technology; the manual digging of postholes represents low technology. A computer-operated numerically controlled milling machine represents high technology in machinery, whereas a carpenter's power saw represents low technology. The higher the technical content of the task, the greater the professionalization and training required of the people who perform the tasks. Research projects that involve complex, nonrepetitive tasks performed by professional workers call for supervisors who function in more of a supportive than a control capacity. Planning formats in research are distinctly different from the flow control that is emphasized in assembly line production.

One of the most potent forces behind both internal and external organizational change is the advance in technology. To stay competitive, firms are required to modify their operations as that technical advance takes place; increased automation is a sufficient example. Automation affects both the people and the structure factors. If machining operations are to be handled by automated equipment, machinists' skills are no longer needed and the machinists are replaced by or converted into maintenance men. That change affects the technical skills required in supervision, and a dramatic impact on structure can also be expected. The formal structure is changed in response to the shift in emphasis from processing to maintenance activities.

When technology changes the skills required in the organization and modifies the physical location of the work stations, it affects worker status and sense of belonging, and causes other traumatic social dislocation in the organization. Advancing technology frequently causes organizational havoc simply because social changes take place far more slowly. Complexity in technology typically results in complexity in management and a more dynamic work environment, both of which spell problems for the manager. Keeping attuned to technological change within an organization is one of the primary concerns of the manager. The technological change tends to alter other aspects of the organization very quickly. It must, therefore, be carefully monitored. It is the regenerative force in many business firms.

The People Factor

People are the key element in any organization. Not only do labor costs normally represent the largest input in any product or service but most management concepts and practices are aimed at better utilization of people. The manager's primary job is, through decision making, to plan, lead, organize, and control the activity in his organization. That puts a premium on ability to motivate, communicate with, and influence employees effectively. In brief, a manager must understand the people in his organization: their level of skill and training, their work attitudes, needs, expectations, goals, and group associations. The better he understands them, the better chance he has of applying the concepts and techniques that will affect performance positively. Being sensitive to people and their needs is one of the primary skills a manager must develop.

Included in Figure 2 are some of the more common dimensions that are used to characterize the employees in an organization. The physical and psychological attributes of both supervisors and subordinates must be considered. Understanding human behavior and motivation are essential to a manager's relationship with people both above and below him in the organization; his very success often hinges on his ability to make such relationships favorable. That ability is essential in his assigning people to perform tasks and getting them to assume responsibilities. Matching the demands of particular jobs with the skills and interests of people is another of the critical aspects of supervision.

The Structure Factor

The structure of the organization is frequently a function of the tasks, technology, and people involved in organization activities; thus it tends to be more of a dependent than independent factor. However, the characteristics of the organization structure have a strong influence on the effectiveness of most management systems and operations.

A good example of the characteristics of structure is scale or size. When an organization is small, verbal communication is adequate in

25

keeping people informed on what is taking place and in knowing the desires of management. However, as the organization becomes larger, more written reports and communications are necessary to maintain the same level of communication. Size similarly affects the detail and complexity of planning and control systems. Simple operations require relatively simple systems—the more numerous and complex the operations, the more complex the systems.

Figure 2. **People factor dimensions.**

DIMENSIONS	MEANS OF EVALUATION
Age	18 70
Physical dexterity	1 (slow) (agile) 10
Reasoning skills	1 (low) (high) 10
Mathematical skills	1 (low) (high) 10
Language skills	1 (low) (high) 10
Other aptitudes	Describe:
Degree of training	1 (little training) (highly trained) 10
Nature of training	Describe: craft, profession, manual tasks, etc.
Leadership skills	Management training and knowledge, attitudes, motivation, etc.
Work attitudes	1 (favorable) (unfavorable) 10
Other psychological factors	Describe and evaluate needs, expectations, roles, goals, values, emotional makeup, group identifications, temperament, interests, etc.

In turn, size affects other dimensions of structure. As organizations grow in size, there is more need for formal procedures to coordinate or integrate activities. Special structures such as committees are needed to integrate the diverse interests represented in the organization. Awkward, ill-conceived, imbalanced formal structures will negatively affect the functioning of every management process and subsystem. Again, structure deserves consideration as one of the key factors in any management situation.

To consider structure only from the standpoint of formal organization is to distort the way in which organizations function. Structure is not exclusively determined by management decisions such as the number of levels in the hierarchy, authority relationships, and functional assignments; it is also determined by social aspects of the organization. The latter are developed through the process of social interaction of the membership. Through the social interaction norms of behavior are developed, status relationships become established, and people assume certain organizational roles. As social systems evolve, they also structure the activities of people and channel human behavior. Thus they constitute powerful forces in organization and management.

FACTORS IN THE ENVIRONMENT

Internal operations aimed at achieving collective organizational goals consistent with institutional purpose are affected by the four primary factors of task, technology, people, and structure. However, the success of an organization in achieving its goals is not entirely a function of how internal operations are managed; it is also a function of adaptation to external forces, organizations, and institutions. A viable organization is a dynamic, changing entity that functions within a dynamic, changing environment. The problem of adaptation to changes in the external environment is another of the basic responsibilities of management. An organization, for example, can be highly efficient in structuring its internal activities to produce a product, but if a competing product is technically superior and lower in cost, the organization may experience failure and its internal efficiency will then go for naught.

External adaptation is not simply a matter of anticipating and reacting to actions of competitors in a particular marketplace. It is also a matter of reacting to and attempting to influence the major forces that generate social change. Those forces are represented by the factors listed in Table 2. The total impact of the external factors on the organization is represented in Figure 3.

The external environment of a firm consists of both forces and institutions. Of most immediate concern to a firm is the market in which it competes. That market is made up of a number of other buyers and sellers who are buying and selling products or services similar to those provided by the firm in question. The firm is also concerned with the marketplace and the environment in terms of inputs it receives from suppliers and skills it receives when it employs people from the labor force. Government agencies, social groups, professional associations, and other institutions are also important parts of the firm's environment.

In addition to institutions, the firm is concerned in a broader sense with the forces and general conditions that exist in its environment at any particular time. Economic trends affect the conditions of the marketplace and, in turn, the condition of the firm. Political, cultural, and technological forces also have both direct and indirect effects on the institutions of the environment (such as competitors, suppliers, customers, government bodies) and therefore on the firm. The environment, then, consists

Table 2. Environmental factors.

Factors	*Dimensions and Means of Evaluation*
Economic	Measurements of economics as a force: Gross national product, personal income, average income, unemployment, sales, profits, size of markets, etc.
	Economic institutions: competitors, suppliers, customers, labor force, business associations, etc.
Political	Political forces: attitudes of public servants, attitudes of major groups and vested interests, public opinion, reactions to events, actions of foreign powers, etc.
	Political institutions: federal, state, local, and foreign governmental bodies and agencies.
Legal	The legal framework within which organizations must function. Laws of federal, state, and local governments. Decisions of courts and quasi-judicial bodies. Decisions of regulatory agencies, etc.
Sociocultural	Sociocultural forces: cultural norms, values of society and subcultures within society, public attitudes, social groups and practices, etc.
Technology	Technology as a force is evaluated and measured by norms associated with each branch of engineering and other applied sciences. Evaluation is in terms of the current state of the art. It is reflected in knowledge and in improvements in machinery, automation, data processing, etc.

Figure 3. **Impact of internal and external factors on the organization.**

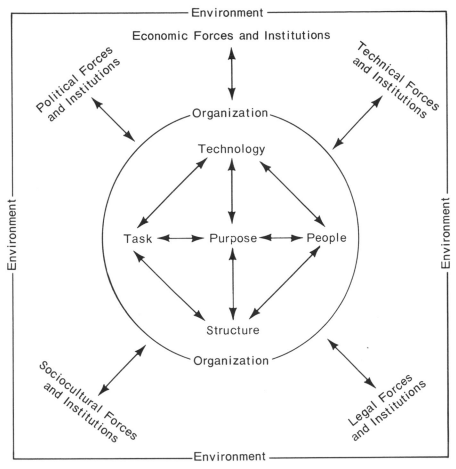

of a mixture of forces, institutions, activities, and events that are inter-related and interdependent. It affects each firm differently because each firm has unique characteristics and a unique interplay of situational factors. In the composite, environmental constraints constitute some of the major factors a manager must work with in planning, formulating policy, and making decisions.

It should be remembered that the forces and institutions in our society are constantly changing and evolving. Since no organization can function apart from its environment, all organizations are affected by changing forces and institutions. Also, since organizations are themselves part of their environment, they contribute to and are part of the forces of change. If, for example, an organization is engaged in research efforts, it not only utilizes scientific knowledge but may also contribute to the stream of scientific discovery.

The Economic Factor

Because the business firm is essentially an economic entity, its activities and results are interwoven with external economic resources, forces, institutions, and conditions. General economic conditions determine the price that a firm must pay for its machinery, material, information, and manpower inputs. The same economic conditions affect the firm's customers and their ability to purchase its goods and utilize its services. Interest rates on money needed for expansion, the market price of securities, and the value of facilities are only a few of the factors affected by economic conditions of the environment. The nature of the market in which the firm competes is also significant. The number and size of buyers and sellers and the degree to which the products are differentiated are two of the market factors that affect the decisions managers must make in both internal and external operations.

Political Factors

Political factors constitute some of the most long-term constraints on the firm. In South America, where political changes are more dynamic than those in the United States, firms are constantly alert to the political climate. A turnover in the party or group in power can result in nationalization. In the more stable political environment of the United States, change is much less extreme but the effects over longer time spans are just as impressive. In recent years the trend has been toward government-business partnerships in major endeavors such as space research. On the other hand, the federal government is taking steps to promote and encourage small business. These and similar trends have major implications for any firm. Thus the actions of politicians, public administrators, legislative bodies, and judicial institutions require the constant awareness of the manager.

Legal Constraints

Closely associated with the political forces in the environment are the legal constraints that both restrict and enhance the activities of a firm. Laws affect all of the major activities of a firm and hence have a dominant role in decision making. People must be hired and employed in accordance with complicated regulations relating to fair employment practices, nondiscrimination, and child labor laws. Products are sold in a marketplace where practices are regulated in accordance with many laws and where activities are scrutinized by many agencies.

Sociocultural Change

The behavior patterns condoned by a group or by society also refuse to remain static. Social institutions and forces are constantly changing and evolving just as the other primary factors in the environment of a firm are. The dramatic changes in clothing styles since World War II are a good example. More subtle but more significant changes are found in the basic values that are at society's foundation. Less emphasis on the value of work, more sexual freedom, and erosion of the respect for authority are only a few of the recent social trends that affect all the institutions of U.S. society, including the business firm.

Technology

As was touched on earlier, technological change has tended to set the pace for economic, social, and even political change. The discovery and utilization of atomic energy, for example, has revised economic, social, and political forces alike. Television too has proved to be an important instrument of economic, social, and political change. Keeping up with technological improvements is one of the prime determinants of the ability of a firm to compete in its market. A firm must ride the forefront of technological advance or its competitors with new or improved products and services will leave it behind. In whole industries such as electronics and aerospace, firms are competitively stratified on the basis of ability to anticipate, generate, and utilize technological improvements. Chapter 6 is devoted to a detailed investigation of technology and its impact on organizations and management operations.

Time Factor

One important factor not reflected in the contingency model so far is the time constraint that affects decision making and the operations of the firm. Every managerial action and decision is influenced by the time frame within which the manager perceives the action and his decision must take effect. Reacting too slowly to external forces can permit competitors to capture a lead in a market; carefully conceived product development and efficient production can be ill-timed, as witness the Edsel; concepts of organization structure, such as decentralization, are affected by the time available for decision making.

Being alert to proper timing in the application of management methods and techniques is another major consideration in the success of management. Every variable in both the internal operations and the external adaptation of an organization is affected by dependent relationships resulting from the time sequencing of events and forces. Timing will therefore be included as one of the major factors in the application of management concepts and techniques in accordance with the contingency approach.

INTERRELATIONSHIP OF THE FACTORS

Two sets of factors in the contingency model of management have now been identified. Internal organization factors consist of the organization's purpose and goals, the people in the organization, the tasks the people are engaged in, the technology of the tasks, and the internal structure. External factors consist of political, social, legal, economic, and technological forces and institutions. Some of the major dimensions by which the factors can be evaluated in any given situation have been identified. However, the manager must do more than identify factors and evaluate them by studying their dimensions; he must weigh the separate intensities and understand the interrelationships of the factors.

No one factor is unaffected by other factors. The relationships may be dependent, independent, or merely associative, but they are never static because organizations, like people, are constantly changing. That holds for the environment of the organization also. The managerial challenge is to understand not only the key variables in the current situation but also the relationships among the variables.

Many examples will be given in the following chapters, but a few are appropriate here. If the tasks necessary to achieve the goals of the organization are complex and upper management hires people with skills not equal to the tasks, there will be a mismatch in those factors and problems will result. If management attempts to build the formal structure of an organization around processes when the tasks naturally lend themselves to a program structure, efficiency will be sacrificed. If an organization is trying to provide improved railroad passenger service when technological and social forces favor automobiles and airplanes, failure will be likely. If tasks are made more specialized, the motivation of the people who perform the tasks will be affected. If an assembly line is further automated but the result is a cost increase that prices the product out of the market, an advance in technology can be disastrous. A manager must therefore know the factors by understanding their dimensions. He needs to appreciate their interrelationships so he can properly select and apply management methods and techniques that will be effective in achieving the results he wants.

The contingency approach to management supports the propositions presented earlier in this chapter. There is no one best way to lead people, organize groups, arrange tasks, or manage an enterprise. Also there is no one best system for planning, controlling, budgeting, coordinating, or integrating the operations of an organization. A manager's effectiveness and the techniques he uses are entirely functions of a properly interpreted situation. The interpretation consists in assessing the primary factors in the situation and then selecting and applying the techniques and methods that are appropriate to the situation as determined by the particular factors.

four
situational methodology and decentralization

BEFORE WE PROCEED with detailed analyses of the factors in the contingency model, a familiarization with situational methodology is necessary. That methodology integrates the concepts and techniques of management with knowledge of the situation. It is the means by which techniques and methods of management are effectively related to the problems a manager faces. That, of course, is the ultimate objective and the culmination of the whole process of applying this management model.

It might appear that the methodology is being presented out of sequence because the primary factors that constitute the contingency model have not been elaborated. However, it is difficult to appreciate the value of the dimensions of each factor unless the way in which the factor affects decision making with situational methodology is known. Therefore the methodology will be elaborated first and its application highlighted later when each of the factors is discussed.

PARTS OF THE METHODOLOGY

Situational methodology involves four steps. For convenience, the steps will be considered sequentially, but in practice the first three are not necessarily sequential but serve more as prerequisites to step 4. The four steps in situational methodology are as follows:

1. *A manager must know of or be familiar with the various concepts and techniques of management that are available.* Before a manager can apply linear programming, decentralization, or network analysis to a situation, he must understand both the technique and its application. That is more difficult than it might at first appear, since hundreds of management concepts, systems, techniques, and methodologies have been developed.

2. *The manager must be knowledgeable of the tradeoffs involved when he selects any particular concept or technique for application.* Each concept is likely to have results that will be both advantageous and disadvantageous to the conditions the manager hopes to establish. Step 2 emphasizes that a manager must not just be familiar with the technique and its underlying concept but should also know what he is buying. He must be familiar with the favorable and unfavorable results that are likely to occur when he pursues a particular course of action.

3. *The manager must know the situation to which he is applying the technique.* He must be familiar with the primary factors in the situation. That familiarity involves an appreciation of the dimensions that affect the status and intensity of each factor. The results achieved by applying any particular management technique will vary with the status of the factors in the situation. For example, to increase the span of control in an organization that is already too loosely administered can only further

weaken the organization, whereas an increase in the span of control in an organization that is overcontrolled is likely to be of benefit.

4. *The manager must not only know the techniques, the tradeoffs related to the techniques, and the particular situation before him but also skillfully match the tradeoffs of the techniques with the needs and demands of the situation.* Developing his skill to such a point that he can effectively relate the tradeoffs and demands is the goal of situational analysis.

In many ways the manager is comparable with a golfer. Just as a golfer must select various clubs to get the ball to the green and into the cup, depending on the course and his lie on it, so the manager must select various techniques that are appropriate to the situation and the dominant factors in it. Both golfer and manager want to progress toward the achievement of objectives. Just as a specific club is selected to meet the needs of a particular lie, so a specific technique is selected to meet the need created by the dominant factors in the situation. The golfer must read the terrain and select a club on the basis of his acquired power and skill; the manager must interpret the situation and select appropriate concepts based on the key variables whose status dictates the effectiveness of the concept to be applied. Being adaptive to the needs of the situation is the objective sought in step 4.

The management concept of decentralization will be used as an example of how situational methodology operates. Decentralization was selected because it is one of the management concepts most widely publicized since World War II and also because it has been so frequently misapplied. There has been a widespread understanding of the concept (step 1) but very frequently a lack of understanding of the full ramifications of implementing the concept (step 2) and sometimes an almost total disregard for the impact that decentralization would have on a particular organization at a specific time (steps 3 and 4).

Before we proceed with a discussion of the tradeoffs of decentralization, a distinction must be made between delegation of authority and decentralization; further, the relative nature of the latter term needs to be accentuated. Delegation of authority is the process by which authority is transferred from one supervisor to another on the next lower level or to a subordinate in his own organization. As top-level managers delegate authority to lower-level supervisors, they add to the decentralization of the organization.

Decentralization is a relative term for the condition of an organization structure when authority has been delegated. If little authority is delegated to lower-level supervisors, the organization structure is said to be centralized; if lower-level supervisors have been delegated considerable authority to make decisions regarding their activities, the organization is said to be decentralized. No organization, of course, is completely centralized or decentralized; each can be classified as representing some point along a centralization–decentralization continuum.

Decentralization can relate to any one of several conditions in an organization: the amount of authority delegated to branches located some distance from the home office, the amount of authority delegated to the lower levels of the hierarchy in one branch at one location, and even the amount of authority that a supervisor delegates to subordinates in his work group. However, our concern here is not with the various forms of decentralization but with the benefits and limitations that derive from its utilization.

A distinction should also be made between decentralization policies and practices. The company policy may call for decentralization, but implementation is strongly affected by the personality, needs, and management philosophy of the individual supervisors. If a supervisor lacks confidence in his subordinates, if he tends not to be a risk taker in respect to letting others make decisions, or if he seeks power to satisfy his own ego needs, he will be inclined to keep his operation centralized. One of the major problems experienced by firms that want more decentralization is to find executives who can make the necessary adjustment in their behavior patterns. Decentralization is a movement toward power equalization, and so it frequently conflicts with the needs and ego drives of strong executives. Here we have a good example of the people factor.

EVALUATION OF DECENTRALIZATION

Certain specific advantages associated with centralization are the corresponding weaknesses of decentralization. Decentralization, on the other hand, has specific benefits that have made it one of the favorite topics of management writers. The specific tradeoffs (step 2) involved in the decision of whether to centralize authority are as follows:

Centralization	*Decentralization*
Achieves conformity and coordination	Reduces load on overburdened executives
Broader, improved decision making	
Avoids suboptimization	Highly motivational for lower supervisors
Improved, balanced, central control	
Permits more staff experts	People are more productive
Avoids duplication	Develops managers, especially general managers
Consistent with needs of leadership	
	Obtains quicker decisions
	Local conditions considered in decision making
	With parallel units can encourage competition

Advantages of Centralization

Bureaucratic and traditional writers on organization say that the primary advantage of centralization is the possibility of exerting more control over and assuring more conformity in the operations performed. In military battles the ground, air, and naval forces must be centrally controlled and coordinated. In somewhat parallel fashion, the advertising campaigns for a company and its products must normally be centrally controlled and coordinated. When conformity and coordination are important in the operations of an organization, centralization of authority is mandatory.

A second advantage of centralization is related to the top executives' skills in decision making. Assuming top executives have the time to make all of the decisions referred to them, they will normally give broader consideration to the interests of the entire organization. Since they establish policy, they will be more familiar with the organization's goals and objectives than will those who only implement policy. Also, by the nature of their responsibilities and their perspective from the top, higher-level managers will consider more factors than will an individual with more limited responsibilities and a lower-level view.

Middle managers who are strongly obsessed with the value of their functional responsibilities frequently make suboptimal decisions or decisions that are optimal to their subgroup but suboptimal to the broader organization. In contrast, top managers are required to consider what is of value for the entire organization and not for just the function they represent. When Robert McNamara was made Secretary of Defense, he found this difference to be one of his major problems. Each military service would approach his office with its own proposals for weapons systems or for projects that it favored to meet an allegedly common defense mission or objective. Since he did not have the information on which to base an evaluation of the conflicting requests, he established a systems analysis group as a part of his office to obtain an independent review of the proposals. Decisions at that level helped avoid duplication and proliferation of weapons systems.

As McNamara stated, "The Secretary of Defense . . . must make certain kinds of decisions, not because he presumes his judgment to be superior to his advisers', military or civilian, but because his position is the best place from which to make these decisions." [1] That approach not only avoids suboptimization but makes possible the attainment of balanced, central control in accordance with the fourth advantage of centralization and the avoidance of duplication in accordance with the sixth one. The more decisions that are left to a variety of subgroups, the more likely will resources and capability be duplicated.

Centralization has an advantage in that it permits the hiring of staff specialists to handle common support functions such as procurement. At lower levels there are not enough resources or activities to warrant the hiring of specialists. Associated advantages often accrue; an example is the quantity discount made possible by central procurement. If all the resources for staff specialists are combined for centralization at the top of an organization, the total is sufficient to provide capability beyond the capacity of any subdivision or branch. For that reason, such functions as long-range planning, product development, marketing research, procurement, finance, and personnel are normally centralized in an organization.

A final advantage of centralization is that it is consistent with the needs and drives of executives at the top of the organization. The power and prestige that are provided the executives may be necessary to sustain leadership in time of crisis or to provide the momentum necessary in an all-out effort to reach an objective. Strengthening leadership by centralization may be necessary in certain circumstances, as when one aspect of the leader's role is the balancing of strong interests within the organization.

Advantages of Decentralization

Studies show that the American executive typically works much longer than the normal 40-hour workweek and often averages upward of 60 hours. More than that, a backlog of work commonly awaits his attention. Proper decentralization can relieve that burden and permit him to direct his efforts at the policy matters that are most critical to the organization.

Perhaps decentralization has as its most important advantage that it is extremely motivational for lower-level supervisors who are given more independence in the work situation. Subordinates can see more directly the results of their efforts and get a greater feeling of accomplishment from their performances if they have more control over what they do. The opportunity to satisfy recognition and self-actualization needs creates strong drives within individuals that normally result in greater commitment to the organization and greater productivity from the individual.

Because management is still primarily an art that is learned by doing, decentralization is important in developing managers. The opportunity to make significant decisions quickly orients the decision maker to the organization's responsibilities and needs. Profit decentralization, for example, has proved valuable in developing general managers. When a manager is made responsible for the entire operation of a plant with only a few primarily financial restrictions, he soon becomes a generalist in balancing the many interests and functions of his organization.

Decentralization leads to quicker decisions. When decision making is centralized, almost all decisions must be referred upward through many channels, which is a slow process. Often the executive who makes the ultimate decision is not acquainted with the local conditions in which the problem originated. When decision-making authority is retained at the lower levels, the organization is usually much more flexible and adaptive.

Finally, decentralization makes possible divisions or other parallel organizational units that perform essentially the same operations and therefore have much the same inputs and outputs. That arrangement is referred to as the deadly parallel because performance comparisons can be made. Not only can performance be easily measured but competitive forces that may improve performance can be encouraged.

SITUATIONAL FACTORS RELATED TO DECENTRALIZATION

The third step in situational analysis is to identify and evaluate the factors that are predominant in the situation. The decision maker must be thoroughly familiar with the people in the organization, the nature of the tasks being performed, the technology of the tasks, the organization structure, and other such factors. He must assess the status of the factors so that he can take the fourth step, which is to match the situation with the techniques that might be applied. The status of certain factors will dictate the selection of certain techniques. Viewed from the opposite direction, the success or failure of the techniques to be applied will be determined by the status of the effective factors in the situation.

Eleven factors constitute the primary constraints that affect the decision whether centralization or decentralization would be most appropriate. They are:

Purpose and goals of the organization.
Scale or size of the organizational structure.
Geographical dispersion of the structure.
Scientific content or the technology of the tasks.
Skill, training, and attitudes of people.
Time frame of the decisions to be made.
Significance of the decisions to be made.
State of the organization's planning and control systems.
State of the organization's information systems.
Degree of conformity and coordination required in the operations.
External environmental factors such as governments and labor unions.

Before we examine each factor, it should be recognized that no single factor or set of two or three factors tends to predominate in influencing decisions on decentralization. A mixture of factors affects the three modes of decentralization discussed earlier. Thus, each factor must be related to both the impact it has individually on the decision to centralize or decentralize and on the composite effect of all of the key factors on the decision.

Purpose and goals of the organization. If a profit-making organization has as a goal a rapid increase in total assets through acquisition and merger with no regard for the product produced, decentralization in operations is necessary. The managers of a conglomerate cannot direct in detail the operations of a large number of subsidiaries with different product lines; no single set of executives has the knowledge necessary to handle such technical diversity. If a firm's goal is to produce only one product, centralization is much more feasible.

Scale dimensions of the structure. Size is a significant factor in decentralization. The larger a firm grows, the less possible it is for one executive or set of executives to make most of the decisions. A drugstore owner with 15 employees to supervise might retain most of the managerial decision making, but in any larger organization with a diversity of people and tasks the supervisor will not have the time or knowledge to retain the same scope of decision making himself.

Geographical dispersion of the structure. A firm with geographically dispersed branches and operations usually requires greater decentralization than one that is more compact. A decision is best made by someone who has the facts relevant to it, and the relevant facts must include the local conditions. Typically, the man directly in charge of the affected operation is best prepared to make a decision concerning it. That makes advisable the delegation of authority to local supervisors in geographically dispersed firms.

Technological content of the tasks. One of the more important trends in organizations since the 1920s is the increased technological complexity of the tasks performed. In the industries of a half century ago, tasks were primarily physical and relatively routine and higher-level supervisors had the knowledge necessary for the direction of a variety of operations. As the work reflected greater complexity because of technological advance, it was no longer possible for a supervisor to exert detailed control over a number of operations. Many technical tasks must be performed by experts in a narrow field of knowledge. Frequently, the expert is so much more knowledgeable of the technical operation than his supervisor that he must be given free rein. With time, an organization's structural hierarchy has come to represent a knowledge hierarchy much less than it once did. The technological status of an organization's operations is thus an important consideration in decentralization.

Skill, training, and attitudes of people. The people factor of decentralization is closely associated with the technology factor. A supervisor's willingness to delegate authority is a function of how successful he feels subordinates will be in decision making. If they are trained and knowledgeable and are committed to the objectives of the company, he will be inclined to delegate; but if for some reason he lacks confidence in their ability to make reasonable decisions, he will continue to make the decisions himself. Of course, decentralization is also a function of the supervisor. His personality must be such that he is willing to let others have a share in the decision making and in the power derived from authority.

Time frame of the decisions. The nature of the operations and the particular situation determine whether decisions need be quick or can be slower and more deliberate. If decisions must be made quickly by individuals in charge of the operations, authority must obviously be delegated to the appropriate individuals. One of the major drawbacks of centralization is that recommendations regarding a necessary decision tend to float upward through many levels to the top of the organization. All such decisions compete with other demands for the time of the central decision maker. Consequently, they are often delayed until their period of usefulness has passed. For example, a forest ranger in charge of a district might find in the spring season that the range is not growing as he anticipated and that campground utilization by tourists is not as he had predicted. If in order to reallocate funds for these two phases of his work he must receive the approval of the National Forest Supervisor, the Regional Director, and then the Forest Service headquarters in Washington, D.C., the growing and tourist seasons might be over before the decisions are made.

Significance of the decisions. Major policy decisions are prerogatives of the leaders of an organization. Decisions that have a major impact on costs are also retained at the top of the organization. In a procurement organization, however, authority to make decisions is frequently stratified at various levels by the cost implications of the decisions.

State of the planning and control systems. As established earlier, a supervisor is usually willing to let subordinates make decisions if he feels they will make knowledgeable ones that are consistent with the plans, goals, and objectives of the organization. If, however, policies, plans, and goals of the organization do not exist or are very nebulous, the subordinate has no guidelines for making his decisions. Therefore, one of the primary prerequisites for decentralization is to establish policies, plans, and goals and see that they are known and accepted by subordinates. Once those things are done, the subordinates can be given some independence. Their activities will be more predictably consistent with the goals sought.

State of the information systems. As has been emphasized, the individual who has the most accurate and current information on a problem should make decisions concerning it. From that follows the argument that, in geographically distributed operations, the man who is aware of local conditions should make the decisions. However, as management information systems (MIS) have become more sophisticated and as electronic data processing has made information more readily available, some experts have predicted that we will see a movement toward centralization or recentralization. The assumption is that MIS will make a broader range of information available on a more timely basis so that top management will be in a better position to make the organization's decisions. MIS certainly increases the feasibility of centralization but not necessarily the desirability. The latter is a function of all of the factors affecting the question and must be determined by situational analysis.

Conformity and coordination required. Conformity in activities can normally be improved if operations are centrally directed. The greater the number of separate groups making decisions, the greater the difficulty of coordinating activities. If, for example, a chain store wants consistent pricing policies in all of its branches, it must centralize pricing at the corporate level. One of the important factors in decentralization is the degree of conformity and coordination necessitated by the nature of the operations and the desires of management.

External environmental factors. Many factors external to the organization can affect a firm's decisions on decentralization. If labor-management agreements call for the negotiation of contracts by national representatives rather than local ones, labor relations will of necessity be centralized. Also, the federal government commonly requires tax and other reports on a corporate rather than divisional basis. Public relations activities too are frequently centralized at the corporate level to have a greater impact on political and social events. Many other external factors encourage centralization.

APPLICATION OF SITUATIONAL ANALYSIS

Proper assessment of the preceding factors is the key to situational analysis. A manager has certain goals and objectives that he is attempting to achieve for his organization. He also has certain knowledge of and experience with a host of management concepts and techniques. However, simply knowing the pros and cons of techniques is not an adequate basis for the selection of any one technique as a means of achieving the desired objectives. The result of the application of any technique is entirely dependent upon the nature of the situation, as defined by the factors of the situation, to which it is applied. Thus the critical step of situational analysis is the final one of matching management concepts and techniques with the factors that dominate the situation to the end of effective progress toward the organization's goals.

In the decentralization example the manager must assess each of the 11 factors in his situation. Certain of the factors may be extremely operative; others may be almost absent. When an organization has weak controls, a lack of direction, few policies, and undertrained lower-level supervisors, the need for centralization is obvious. When it has over-burdened executives, dispersed operations, diversified products, a well-trained staff, and extensive technology, the need for decentralization is equally obvious. Rarely, however, are all the factors so tilted in one direction; normally they will indicate a conflict in guidelines. A company may at the same time need more conformity and coordination in its activities but also have morale problems because not enough authority is delegated to lower-level supervisors. Typically, one benefit has to be gained at the expense of another.

Certain functions do tend to be more centralized or decentralized be-cause of the characteristics of the operations. Finance functions are typically centralized because of their importance to top management. They constitute one of the primary organizational controls, and they bear on top-management responsibility for resource allocation. Personnel functions are also often centralized to insure wage and salary equity and the success of middle- and top-management staffing. Operations decisions are typically decentralized when managers familiar with local circum-stances can make better decisions.

Situational analysis is thus an exercise in identifying, weighting, and evaluating each factor that is significant in a specific situation and then selecting the applicable concepts and techniques. In the instance of decentralization, situational analysis is normally a matter of assessing the 11 factors to determine whether authority should be decentralized or further delegated in an organization. Many would argue that the analysis is much too complex. However, as John J. Morse and Jay W. Lorsch state after a major study of organizations, "The strength of the contingency approach . . . is that it begins to provide a way of thinking about this complexity rather than ignoring it." [2] Undoubtedly situational analysis is complex; but if it is properly undertaken, it forces a balanced, thorough decision-making process. Above all, it takes the study of man-agement away from a set of rules and toward a method of analysis.

five
situational management and systems theory

IN RECENT YEARS systems theory has been a major influence toward the modification of traditional management theory. It has been a recent common practice in many disciplines, such as engineering, sociology, and psychology, to apply general systems theory to the knowledge in that field. Such applications have fostered many interesting developments that have tended to result in new understanding and a beneficial integration of knowledge within a discipline. General systems theory has had a major impact on management thought since about 1960. Many of the basic concepts of systems theory are common to situational analysis also, and for that reason the theory deserves special consideration here.

General systems theory offers an approach to reexamining and reanalyzing the knowledge in any particular discipline. The theory includes many tenets and principles, but it does not constitute a new and separate appendage of highly esoteric knowledge. Instead, it is concerned with integrating existing knowledge. That is one of the reasons why it has such a dramatic impact on the disciplines to which it is applied. As systems writers in management emphasize, it is in essence a way of thinking, a way of comprehending and utilizing in a much broader fashion all of the existing knowledge of management.

DEFINITIONS OF SYSTEMS THEORY

Caution is necessary in dealing with definitions of systems theory because any particular definition takes on different meanings depending on whether it is applied to physical, mechanical, social, open, or one of the many other systems in the different bodies of knowledge. Because systems theory was applied to engineering several years before it was applied elsewhere, the engineering definitions are often used. The results, especially when the definitions are applied to organization theory, are misleading. Engineering definitions highlight the position and mechanical functioning of physical parts. They therefore have little direct relation to an organization, which lacks physical parts. Hence the definitions used here are those specifically adopted to have maximum relevance to management systems.

Professors Richard A. Johnson, Fremont E. Kast, and James E. Rosenzweig, who in 1963 wrote one of the first books in which systems theory was applied to management, define a system as "an organized or complex whole; an assemblage or combination of things or parts forming a complex or unitary whole." [1] R. L. Ackoff, who writes from a management science standpoint, defines a system as "any entity, conceptual or physical, which consists of interdependent parts." [2] A system consists of essentially three such parts: a set of elements, relationships among the elements, and a whole integrated from the elements and their relationships. In this book, for that reason, a system will be considered to be an entity consisting of a composite whole that is formed of interdependent parts or elements the relationships of which contribute to the unique characteristics of the whole.

In the original application of systems theory, the parts were physical and the relationships focused on the patterns of the parts. Also, closed physical systems involve the concept of internal structure, since "closed system" implies little interchange of energy or materials with the world outside the system. Thus physical positioning, physical boundaries, and structural patterns receive the primary attention. In an open system, on the other hand, there is an exchange of materials or energies with outside systems or the environment, and so the boundaries of the system are said to be permeable. Furthermore, in open systems, such as organizations, the relationships among the elements are a matter not of physical positioning but of flows or exchanges. Static relationships either internally or externally are uncommon phenomena.

In an open system growth, decay, and adaptation processes dominate. All of the primary factors in an organization are in a constant state of change. The workers and their attitudes are not the same from day to day; the leadership is not the same; technology is constantly being updated; and new social relationships are developed among the people in the organization. Externally the marketplace is changing, the status of the economy is in a constant state of flux, and political events and power struggles create a new complexion as each day passes. The assuredness of change is perhaps the most highly predictable feature of open, human systems.

Management systems become quite complex because they have both physical and human elements. In a production plant one of the most important factors in efficient operation is the quality of the physical parts—machines, materials, and processing equipment—and their physical patterning along a production line. Each part that contributes to the manufacture of the end item must be combined with other parts in a closely coordinated and integrated way if the plant or system is to be effective. Also, the purely open system aspects of a production plant involving the members of the workforce and their interrelationships must be taken into consideration if the plant—the whole—is to be effective.

Systems theory holds that to describe what a manager does or what management processes are is not enough: To have a thorough understanding of any situation, it is necessary to understand the primary factors in that situation and their interrelationships. Not surprisingly, systems theorists are critical of traditional management theory; for that theory has been built by identifying what managers do and what the management processes are. The resulting contribution to understanding is relatively superficial. If someone is to affect a situation, he must understand how the current conditions came into being, and that requires an understanding of cause-and-effect relationships. Ultimately that involves a knowledge of the primary factors in a situation and of the relationships among those factors. Now the close tie between systems theory and situational analysis becomes apparent. Both go beyond descriptive knowledge to a search for the prime factors in each situation and the relationships among the factors.

Systems theory is also a reaction to the scientific method, whose application has divided subject matter and research into smaller and smaller segments. Research and analysis are directed at acquiring highly detailed information. Systems theorists agree that such information is valuable, but they point out that its worth cannot be fully comprehended until it is related to the larger system of which it is a part. They contend that too often our analysis is confined and narrow; it is parts-oriented rather than whole-oriented.

Systems theory supports a search for the broad understanding that comes from identifying the major entities that constitute systems and from an understanding of the relationships of those entities that give systems their unique characteristics. Separate phenomena cannot be properly understood in isolation because all matter and information is in some way related to other matter and information.

Examples of Systems

One or two examples will serve to illustrate systems theory. As noted earlier, the theory was first applied in engineering, and much of the publicity about systems had to do with U.S. weapons systems since World War II. Prior to the war integrating the parts of a weapons system was a rather minor technical problem, because the weapon was apt to be some kind of gun and its ammunition. When after the war advanced technology produced highly complex weapons, the problem of systems integration became much more severe. A missile carrying a nuclear warhead has thousands of parts that often are fabricated by thousands of contractors. And even if all of those parts are properly positioned and integrated so that the missile will function as prescribed, the missile itself is still only a part of the total weapon system.

For the total system to function as designed, each of its parts must perform effectively. If a missile is effective but the ground silo or the submarine from which it is to be fired is not properly sized to handle the missile, the weapon system as a whole will not function. The parts of a weapon system that must integrate perfectly for objective accomplishment include all of the components of the missile, the handling harnesses and transportation equipment used to move the missile, the physical facilities for storing and firing the missile, and the training manuals needed by the personnel who will transport, maintain, and fire the missile.

All the system parts, then, must be properly interrelated if the total system is to function. Here enters the systems engineer. He does not design individual parts, but he does insure that they are designed in such a way that they contribute to the successful functioning of the total system. If any one part is changed, the ramifications of the change must be tracked down. All other parts and the functioning of the total system must be considered, since the relationship can have a dependent effect on the other parts of the system.

A human organization has equally intricate relationships. To really know who has power in an organization, it is necessary to know many other things: the kinds of people in the organization and their knowledge and personality and formal positions, the group norms and goals, and the relationships among individuals and among subgroups. It is this variety of relationships that produces the composite whole of the organization and its power structure. If only one aspect of the power relationships—perhaps authority-based power—is understood, comprehension of the power structure as such is impossible because that aspect is only one factor of many. Any company or even any product line is a composite of many parts and factors that must be understood individually and by their interrelationships before the whole can be comprehended in other than a superficial, descriptive fashion.

SEVEN CONCEPTS THAT CONSTITUTE SYSTEMS THEORY

To repeat, systems theory is not a discrete body of knowledge; it is the basis of a method for putting existing knowledge in a different perspective. For that reason it is often nebulous and hard to understand until considerable time is spent in working with the concepts. Our current approaches to knowledge are so stereotyped that it is difficult to perceive the same knowledge from a different standpoint. However, systems theory does consist of a limited number of principles that are an aid in this new way of thinking. The seven principles of systems theory that relate to open, social systems are as follows:

1. All the parts of a system are interdependent.
2. The whole is more than a summation of the individual parts (synergy).
3. To properly understand the parts it is first necessary to understand the whole (holism).
4. Boundary relationships and interfaces are critical in understanding the nature of a system.

5. Each system is one level in a hierarchy of systems.
6. Open systems are viable, changing entities.
7. An open system has the ability to transform resources and avoid the decay process of physical systems (negative entropy).

Each of the principles is extremely important to systems theory and therefore deserves elaboration.

Dependency of Parts

Interdependency, the first characteristic of systems theory, is most often used to identify a system. Is there a dependent relationship among the parts? What is the whole that owes its existence to the interdependent parts? If an element has no impact upon an entity and if the entity does not in turn rely on it for its functioning, then the element is not part of the system. If a change in one part affects other parts and, in turn, the whole, then the part is an element of the system and the system behaves coherently as a whole.

The contingency model presented in Chapter 3 is based upon the interdependency concept. Organizations consist of people, tasks, structure, technology, and common purposes. The functioning of the organization is dependent on the relationship among those components. If one part such as leadership (people factor) changes, the change affects the whole, the entire organization; if the purpose and task (system parts) of the organization are modified, the functioning of the whole organization is affected. Each factor has some impact on other factors and thus on the whole. One of the primary challenges of systems theory is to identify a specific entity as a system and to comprehend how each part contributes to the maintenance, adaptation, or functioning of the whole. The insight that accompanies the understanding is one of the primary benefits of systems theory.

Synergy and the Functioning of the Whole

Synergy is the simultaneous action or operation of separate but interrelated parts producing a total effect greater than the sum of the effects taken independently. If an engine is disassembled, the parts still exist but are no longer properly interrelated; the system no longer exists. There are no composite, unique attributes of the whole because a whole does not exist. However, when the engine is reassembled and the parts are again properly interrelated, the engine functions; it has characteristics and an output that are distinct from the characteristics of the individual parts. The important point regarding wholes is that they are not simply aggregates or summations of parts. The number of parts of an engine, whether assembled or disassembled, is the same; the interrelationship makes the difference.

A similar example can be based on people working in a group. If five individuals coordinate their activities and work in unison, the effect or output will be considerably different than if the same five people work independently in an unrelated fashion. Again the key point is that it is impossible to understand wholes by breaking them down and studying the parts. The uniqueness of the whole is created not by the individual parts but by the relationships among the parts. In human organizations conflict relationships among the participants will produce a different organization and a different output than will cooperative relationships. The parts may be the same, but the relationship is different. Synergy, therefore, focuses on the basic management responsibility for properly interrelating the parts of a system and thereby maximizing the output of the system.

Holism and the Functioning of Parts

Holism is closely related to synergy, and some would even argue that the two concepts are the same. However, synergy has to do with the unique features or characteristics of the functioning whole, and holism with the functioning and features of the parts as they relate to the whole or totality. The essence of the holism concept is that a system can be explained only as a totality. Just as an understanding of the whole depends on a comprehension of the relationships among the parts and the synergistic effect of that relationship, so the complete understanding of a part depends on a comprehension of what that part contributes to the whole. To understand the independent functioning or characteristics of the part is not to know the part. The way to know the part is to understand the whole and what the part contributes to the synergistic phenomenon of the whole.

That brings us back to the same lesson. To study phenomena in isolation or to describe the attributes of existing phenomena is too limited to be useful. Complete understanding comes only from a knowledge of relationships. If a manager understands only the tasks performed in the organization and does not understand the people who perform the tasks, then he cannot possibly understand the interrelationship of those two factors. Yet the interrelationship itself has the primary effect on the output of the operation.

A manager cannot just know one factor in a situation. If he is to understand the situation, he must understand both the factors and interrelationships that determine the significant characteristics of the whole. The significance of a factor in a situation can be understood only by knowing the relationship of that factor with other factors and with the whole situation.

Boundary Relationships

The boundary relationships of physical systems are obviously important because of the significance that structure has for physical systems. Such boundaries are discrete and easy to identify; they constitute the interface of the physical entity with other systems and with phenomena exterior to the system. In contrast, boundaries in open, social systems are rarely discrete, and they are much harder to identify. Furthermore, the boundaries in an open system are by definition permeable to energy, materials, and information that are exchanged with other systems and with the environment. In fact, the permeability of the boundaries is one of the distinctive features of an organization; the ease with which someone can become part of an organization is one of its primary social characteristics. Communication, interaction, and exchange of resources are affected by the boundary conditions of an organization.

One of the values of the boundary principle of systems theory is that it warns the manager to be concerned with the boundaries of his organization, its interfaces with other systems and with external factors. The handling of those interfaces often determines the success or failure of the firm. The key interfaces of a business firm are its relationships with its customers, suppliers, and other outside groups such as the local community, governments, unions, and professional organizations. Unless an organization can maintain favorable relationships with those groups it cannot achieve its goals as a system.

Traditional management focuses primarily on how to structure the internal operations of a firm to maximize productive efficiency. Systems theorists emphasize that the firm's external relations are as important as or more important than its internal operations. A firm can be extremely efficient internally but it will fail if its external policies have alienated its customers or other outside groups with which it must work to survive. Productive efficiency will represent the optimization of a part but the suboptimization of the whole if balance is not maintained in all of the firm's vital functions and relations.

There is little doubt that many of the most important decisions a manager has to make are those related to the boundary conditions of the organization. Accordingly, the contingency model consists of two sets of factors. People, tasks, technology, purpose, and structure are the internal factors, and economic, political, technical, sociocultural, and legal forces and institutions are the external factors. No attempt is made to assess the relative importance of the two sets of factors. Since the internal factors are much more subject to control by the manager, they are given far greater attention in management literature. Accordingly, the systems model is a much broader and better balanced concept of the firm than is to be found in traditional management writings.

The Hierarchy of Systems

A principle closely related to the boundary one is that any system is only one level in a hierarchy of systems. All knowledge, all information, and all activity are grouped into systems of varying complexity. Nature is a vast fabric of related and unrelated systems. In any particular discipline or area of knowledge, there are lower-level elements that constitute the basic systems of that discipline. Other systems of increased complexity at higher levels have the lower-level systems as subsystems of the suprasystem. Thus hierarchies of systems tend to dominate nature in regard to both closed and open systems.

One of the landmarks in the development of systems theory was an article written in 1956 by Kenneth Boulding, an economist. Boulding attempted to divide all knowledge of the universe into a nine-level hierarchy.[3] On the first level are static systems, such as the anatomy of the universe. Each succeeding level in the hierarchy represents an increase in complexity. For example, on levels four through six are biological systems; on level seven is the human system; on level eight are the social systems; and on level nine are transcendental systems.

The hierarchy concept is useful because it acknowledges interaction not only within a system and among systems on the same level but also vertically among systems on different levels. If a particular level in the hierarchy is taken as reference, there can be subsystems and subsubsystems of that system as well as suprasystems and suprasuprasystems. The relationships that exist in nature are not limited to the parts of a system; they are found among the systems existing both as subsystems of a system and as broader-level systems external to the system. Such systems subordinate, constrain, or enhance the focal systems. Their relationships are thus of concern to the manager.

Systems theorists have provided little elaboration of the hierarchies as they are related to open, social systems, but the hierarchy concept as it is related to formal organization structure is a part of every manager's experience. The primary work group is at the lowest level, and top-level management is at the apex. Thomas A. Petit has gone beyond this to designate a four-step hierarchy consisting of the technical core, organizational level, institutional level, and environment of the firm.[4] In viewing the hierarchy concept from the standpoint of the practitioner, however, six levels of open, social systems become evident when the focal system is considered to be the firm:

1. The individual, the operations level.
2. The primary work group, including both formal and informal groups.
3. The basic functional organization: production, engineering, accounting, etc.

4. The institutional level, the firm.
5. The competitive system, the marketplace.
6. The environmental level, including the situational factors of technical, political, economic, sociocultural, and legal forces and institutions.

The basic element of a social system is, of course, the individual, and the next level in the social hierarchy consists of groups of individuals. The primary work group and informal groups to which an individual belongs constitute the most elementary groups in the firm. They are collected into larger organizational entities, typically on a functional or professional basis that represents the skill specialization of the individuals involved. However, the next higher level might consist of subgroups identified with products, processes, or other forms of departmentation; this is level 3. The intermediary organizations are then combined together and managed for the purpose of meeting the objectives of the focal organization, which is called the institutional level and consists in our example of the firm.

Levels 5 and 6 comprise the environmental systems that are external to the firm. The marketplace of the firm functions as a system. The number of buyers and sellers, the basis on which the firms compete, the strategies of the firms, the nature of the products, and the basic economic forces of supply and demand affect the suprasystem. Level 6, the environmental level, consists of the basic national and international forces of a political, economic, sociocultural, legal, or technological nature. Those forces affect all lower-level systems through the pervasive influence they have on all the social systems existing as part of the world society.

Many benefits can come from viewing a firm as part of a hierarchy and examining the relationships among the various levels of the hierarchy. On each of the first four levels are social systems that have separate goals, many of which conflict with the goals of systems at other levels. Role conflict and conflict among groups can be more easily comprehended in that framework. Also, the supervisor, as the man in the middle, can be seen as subject to the forces that impinge upon him from supra- and subsystems. Significant relationships among the different levels of the hierarchy influence attitudes and activities of individuals and groups and must therefore be considered by the manager.

The hierarchy concept of systems is further complicated by vertical subsystems. Most management subsystems are of that kind. The planning, control, communication, and organization subsystems are established by management to tie together the various levels of the organization. They cut vertically through the levels of internal hierarchy with the objective of integrating the activities of the organization to achieve the goals of the institution, the fourth level in the hierarchy.

There is, of course, no known orderly table or matrix that neatly ties all social systems together. The unique characteristics of each system make generalization in broad terms necessary. Social systems often exist in what could be considered almost a complete disarray with little evidence of a finite hierarchy. However, the important thing is to consider groups as social systems in which internal and external relationships are considered as systems relationships. Such relationships have many implications derived from the concepts of systems theory provided in this chapter.

THE NATURE OF SOCIAL SYSTEMS

One of the most important characteristics of open, social systems is their changing, viable nature. Philip Selznick, a sociologist, emphasized the organic, adaptive nature of organizations more than a quarter century ago. In none of its features does an organization tend to remain fixed; it is constantly redefined by both internal and external forces. The external forces—economic, technological, political, and social—are themselves in a constant state of change.

The continued existence of an organization is frequently a function of how it responds to the forces on it. Traditional management theory has relied on the bureaucratic model of organization developed at the turn of the century by Max Weber. That is the stable, mechanistic approach to organizations. Systems theory, on the other hand, embodies the organic approach; it starts with the changing, variable nature of the environment and attacks the problem of adaptation that faces an organization if it is to survive. Certainly business firms cannot ignore social, political, economic, and technological forces. Some organizations are, of course, more directly affected by them than others, but success in the marketplace normally depends on riding the forefront rather than clinging to the coattail of change.

Negative Entropy

Closed physical systems are characterized by entropy. They cannot replenish their energy, and so a decay process sets in. The result is a movement toward disorder, lack of resource transformation, and eventual death or destruction. In contrast, living systems survive by importing materials from their environment and transforming those materials into energy. They thereby avoid decay. The problem of open systems, then, is to arrest entropy (negative entropy) and avoid disorder and destruction. That agrees with the input-output model of economics. Materials, energy, and information are imported into the firm; there they are transformed into goods and services. The outputs are then distributed in the marketplace, the environment.

Biological systems never manage perfect negative entropy. For long periods of time they import sufficient resources from the environment to grow and expand, but eventually they are subject to deterioration and death. Theoretically, however, organizations can escape that fate; in theory they are capable of functioning indefinitely by replenishing their resources. That success is a function of adaptation. If an organization does not adapt to external forces, it can quickly go out of existence; the statistics on small-business mortality are grim testimony. Negative entropy in regard to organizations makes it mandatory that leadership be concerned with adaptation to the factors that are significant in the firm's environment.

SITUATIONAL ANALYSIS AND SYSTEMS THEORY

Situational analysis has very greatly benefited by the redirection given management theory and practice by systems theory since the early 1960s. In many respects some of the key concepts of situational analysis have grown out of earlier concepts developed as a result of a systems approach to management. In particular, the indebtedness of situational analysis is to two of the broader concepts of systems theory. One relates to the internal operations of the firm and the other to the external. In the systems theory concept of internal management, the manager concentrates on the relationships of the parts of the organization and knows what those relationships mean to the functioning of the whole. In situational analysis the fundamental concept is to know the primary factors and their interrelationships, since they constitute the variables with which the manager must deal if he is to affect the current situation. Both concepts avoid descriptive analysis and concentrate on factors, relationships of factors, and a search for underlying causes.

The systems theory concept that has the greatest bearing on the external aspect of situational analysis is that an organization is a changing, dynamic, social system with the primary problem of adapting to external forces and institutions. Management theory and writing have been too concentrated on the problem of internally structuring a firm to maximize efficiency. The emphasis on the management role of adapting the organization to external forces and institutions has tended to correct that deficiency. In situational analysis the problem of adaptation is highlighted by dividing all the factors into two categories, internal and external. Then the effort is to identify the factors that are most operative in the situation and therefore most involved in the adaptation process.

The tie between situational analysis and systems theory is extremely important. Systems theory is not necessarily the forerunner of situational analysis, nor is situational analysis a mere handmaiden of systems theory. Although the two have some of the same roots, they have distinctive contributions to make. From the way they complement each other, it could be said that they have a synergistic effect on management theory and practice.

six
task and technology factors

OF THE FIVE primary internal factors, only three are to be examined in detail: task, technology, and organization structure. The purpose and people factors are excluded from detailed coverage either because their significance as factors is obvious or because their dimensions have been thoroughly investigated in other management literature. The purpose factor is excluded primarily for the first reason. To say again that an organization with profit as a long-range goal and production of a specific product as an intermediate goal is dominated by production tasks and efficiency psychology is hardly necessary. However, even though it is apparent that the basic purposes and goals of an organization will dictate the tasks performed and will attract people of specific skills, interests, and value systems, one should not therefore underestimate the complexity or importance of the observation.

Organizations with different goals and purposes will function in different ways. A government agency attempting to achieve certain conditions in society through the services it provides will engage in different tasks, use different criteria in decision making, and be composed of a different set of employees than an industrial firm attempting to optimize its profit through the sale of its products. A religious organization, again, will function differently because of its unique goals and tasks and the particular attitudes of its membership. Many of the primary differences in organizations and their management can be traced back to the basic purposes for which the organizations exist. Goals are important not only because they have a deterministic effect on other variables but also because they are a part of the management processes of planning, leading, and motivating. Goals are both a factor and a management tool. As a management tool they are exemplified by the highly successful management-by-objectives programs.

People as a factor in situational analysis need no detailed coverage because their influence and attributes are obvious and because so much management literature has already been written about human behavior and human relations. To state that people have different aptitudes, interests, attitudes, and levels of training and that because of those differences a manager must deal with them in different ways is again to state the obvious. Specifically how those differences affect the way in which supervisors should deal with subordinates, involving, as it does, application of concepts and methods of management, is another matter. It is covered in Chapters 9 and 10 on leadership styles and motivation. The dimensions or attributes of people are well recognized by managers and require no further explanation, given what is our immediate purpose here—understanding the relationship among the factors in the contingency model.

TECHNOLOGY AND TASK CONSIDERATIONS

The topics for this chapter are the technology and task factors. The two are considered together because of their close relationship; as was noted earlier, sociologists and others commonly use the terms as synonyms. However, the two are separated in this analysis to give greater emphasis to the technical content of tasks performed in organizations. In Chapter 3 tasks are defined as the activities in which people are engaged when they belong to an organization or when they are acting on behalf of the organization. They comprise assigned duties or expected behavior patterns as determined by the people who are members of or participants in the organization. Series of tasks constitute the work flow of the organization. If part of the work flow is handled by machines, that part is properly referred to as processes or machine processes rather than tasks.

Technology represents the intellectual content of a task or series of tasks; it is most commonly thought of as the degree of sophistication of the mechanical or machine aspect. Also, since the early 1800s, it has increasingly been identified with applied science. If tasks are basically routine, physical, and lacking in stringent mental demands, they represent elementary technology. If they are more complicated and involve complex, systematized knowledge of a profession or if they require utilization of sophisticated machinery, they are high on the technology scale.

A close relationship between tasks and technology is inevitable because both are integral parts of the organization's activities. If the organization's goals involve the production of a product, production tasks are designated. Those tasks are associated with production technology, and the determinants of the technology are the knowledge and financial resources of the organization. Once a production line is in existence, however, the independent factor may be the technology. If, as in the example of Chapter 3, a firm decides to increase the technology of part of its production line, the skills required and the tasks involved may change from production processing to equipment maintenance. Thus a change in tasks is necessitated by a change in technology.

Generally, the two factors have a high associative relationship. If a firm enters the electronics field, a particular mix of tasks and technology is needed; if a group of individuals form a bowling team, other tasks and technology are involved; an accountant for the Internal Revenue Service is engaged in still other tasks and relies on still other technologies. In each instance technology and tasks are closely associated. Our primary concern, however, is how tasks and technology differences affect management decision making. The positions of electronics engineer, bowler, and accountant are unique for the primary reason of the difference of tasks in which the individuals are engaged and the difference in intellectual input of the tasks. Those differences have many meanings for the structure, people, leadership, and management of each organization.

SIGNIFICANCE OF THE TASK FACTOR

Tasks are important in management and situational analysis because:

- Tasks are the basic building blocks of job design and personnel administration.
- Tasks are the basic building blocks of organization structure.
- Tasks are prime determinants of people requirements.
- Tasks are one of the primary factors affecting productivity and goal achievement.
- Tasks and task structure strongly affect the motivation and commitment of people.
- Modification of tasks and task structure constitutes one of the most potent means a manager has to institute change in an organization.

Tasks in Personnel Administration

Personnel specialists have traditionally been the ones who give primary attention to tasks in management study. They have viewed tasks as the basic building blocks of job design and job descriptions. A job description constitutes a clustering of tasks that are to be performed by an individual. When all the tasks of an organization have been included in job descriptions, the entire personnel structure has been established. Job specifications can be written to indicate the human qualifications required by the jobs; they then serve as guides for the recruitment and placement of personnel. In addition, wage and salary structures can be established, career ladders outlined, performance standards developed, incentive pay systems set up if they are appropriate, and training needs specified. Essentially, every element of the personnel function in an organization starts with the tasks of the organization as the basic unit.

Tasks and Organization Structure

One of the basic issues that remains unresolved is whether an organization should be established from the top down or from the bottom up. In the first approach the basic functions are divided into smaller and smaller groups until the primary work units are established. In the bottom-up approach the tasks are grouped into jobs and into work units that are eventually combined in a hierarchical fashion. Actually, sound organization planning is based on both approaches. In general, the role of tasks in determining and affecting the efficiency of organization structure has not received the consideration it deserves.

Several writers and researchers have contended that tasks are the primary determinants of organization structure. Eliot D. Chapple and Leonard Sayles were among the first to hold that view. In 1961 they emphasized that the bottom of the organization is where the work is done and so cannot be ignored in structuring an organization. In their opinion, the tasks at the primary work level are the most important factor in organization design, which, they say, should be "based on the actual work flow within a technological and procedural framework."[1]

One of the most comprehensive studies on tasks and technology was undertaken by Joan Woodward and associates in England in the mid-1950s. The project involved an intensive study of 110 British manufacturing companies. The firms were divided into three categories related to unit production, mass and batch production, and process production. One of the major conclusions of the study was that the three different technologies are associated with different features of organization structure.

The conclusion that there is a very close tie between technology, as the Woodward group defines it, and organization structure is a little questionable because at least three major factors are evident in the categories established for the study. They are the task and technology factors as defined in this book and also the size of the organizations resulting from the nature of the technology in the three-category grouping. In the Woodward studies the features of organization structure that differed with the three technology categories were span of control, the number of levels in the hierarchy, the use of committees, and other closely associated factors. The main finding of the study was that "there are prescribed and functional relationships between structure and technical demands."[2]

The findings of other researchers agree with those of Woodward and her colleagues. Arthur H. Walker and Jay W. Lorsch concluded from their studies that if a plant's tasks are routine and repetitive, a functional structure is appropriate, whereas if the task is of a problem-solving nature, ". . . the production organization seems to be more appropriate."[3] Sociologist Charles Perrow has concluded that "technology is a better basis for comparing organizations than the several schemes which now exist."[4] It should be remembered that Perrow uses the sociologist's definition of technology, which is "the work done in organizations."

The relationship between tasks and formal organization structure is also supported by the logic of the traditional organization concept of departmentation. Departmentation is the process of dividing the work and functions of the organization into units such as branches and divisions. The usual recognized forms of departmentation are functional, product or program, process, customer, and territory or geographical. In an oil refinery, where the basic tasks and work flow are established by a continuous operation, one would expect a process form of departmentation. In a firm doing aerospace work, in which all of the tasks to be performed are specified by a contract with the government, one would expect a product or program form of departmentation. In a retail store, where all of the selling tasks are customer-oriented, one would expect a customer form of departmentation. In each instance the basic work to be performed, consistent with the purpose and objectives of the organization, dictates or at least restricts the types of departmentation that are appropriate.

Before we leave the subject of tasks and organization structure, it should be noted that tasks affect informal structure or social structure as well as the formal structure established. Chapple and Sayles provide very convincing arguments in this regard. They state:

> The human relationships within the organization structure do not occur in a vacuum. The patterns they follow, in fact, their very existence, are determined in large part by the techniques, processes, spatial layout, paper systems, etc., that carry out the purpose of the organization and make up the sequences or flows of contacts between people. These technical patterns determine where individuals come into contact, in what order, how often, and for how long; hence serve to facilitate or hinder the interaction between individuals. They control the interaction patterns comprised in the organizational structure, just as the test tubes and complicated glass linkages of the chemistry laboratory control the rates at which chemical processes can occur. To perform a different experiment using the same compounds, the chemist changes his arrangement of tubes, beakers, and piping. Any change in the technical elements that alters the flow of contacts also changes the organizational relationships of the individuals involved, even though the personalities are the same.[5]

Tasks and People

The third reason why tasks are important is that they strongly affect the people factor. It should be remembered that the people factor covers all the human requirements in an organization: the top and middle managers, the first-line supervisors, and all of the subordinates or workers. The diagram indicates the relationship of purpose, technology, task, people, and structure factors.

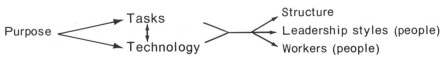

To a degree, an organization's basic purpose dictates its tasks and technology. Since tasks and technology are closely associated, their composite effect is a significant deterministic influence on structure, leadership styles, and workers. The relationship with workers is obviously direct. For example, a marketing organization has as its basic purpose the selling of specific products to customers. That establishes selling tasks as the primary ones of the organization. The job specifications for someone to perform selling tasks call for experience, aptitudes, interests, and certain personality characteristics that have been found to be common to successful salesmen. Similarly, production tasks call for individuals with production skills, training, and interests and welfare organizations call for individuals with social service skills, training, and interests. People requirements in the form of job specifications follow the basic tasks to be performed. Matching the demands of a job with an individual's abilities is one of the primary responsibilities of a manager.

Tasks are also one of the important factors that affect the success of managers with different leadership styles. The basic tasks of an organization and how they are structured affect certain other variables and create certain situations in which some kinds of leaders are more effective than others. That will be dealt with in detail in Chapter 9, but at this point the excellent studies by Fred Fiedler are relevant. Fiedler summarized his and other studies in 1967; his book, *A Theory of Leadership Effectiveness,* is the most important work to date on the contingency concept as it relates to leadership. Here is a significant conclusion of his studies:

> Structured tasks, as exemplified by production management or the day-to-day supervision of relatively unskilled work groups, appear to call for task-oriented leadership; relatively unstructured second-level management functions or higher management, as exemplified by policy making groups and research units of organizations, seem to call for relationship-oriented leadership.[6]

Repetitive, unchallenging tasks require relatively close—that is, task-oriented—supervision. More complex, challenging tasks are typically more psychologically rewarding and motivational, so that close supervision is not as mandatory and relationship-oriented leaders are therefore effective. The nature of tasks and the way in which they are structured in organizations tend to generate certain forces that are best handled by leaders who have styles consistent with the needs of the situation.

Tasks and Productivity

Since the time of Frederick Taylor efficiency specialists have attempted to structure and sequence tasks in an organization to maximize coordination and productivity. They have also sought to reduce energy and resource utilization to the minimum level necessary to achieve the desired objectives. Although in recent years the trend has been to give greater consideration to other objectives, responsibilities, and needs of organization, the basic managerial role remains that of efficiently and effectively achieving organizational objectives. Accordingly, the fourth reason why tasks are important to a manager is that the way in which tasks are structured and sequenced in an organization is one of the primary determinants of productivity. Methods analysis, efficiency standards, and production planning techniques are important tools of the manager.

Tasks and Motivation

The fifth reason why tasks are important to the manager is closely associated with the fourth one. The nature and sequencing of the tasks performed by an individual are among the most significant factors that affect job satisfaction, commitment, motivation, and skill utilization. That has been one of the favorite themes of behavioral scientists since the 1950s. The argument is that the emphasis of production management on job specialization has made jobs too routine, too repetitive, and too shallow for human beings who are seeking a feeling of achievement in their work experiences.

Many psychologists and writers have attacked specialization as making jobs so dull and boring that they arouse feelings of alienation and frustration in the workers. They have urged that jobs be made more challenging and more psychologically rewarding by applying principles of job enlargement and job enrichment. Those two principles will be considered in some detail in Chapter 10; here our concern is to note that no motivational factor is more important than the nature of the task. Therefore, task structure and sequencing take on special significance for the manager.

Tasks and Change

Finally, tasks are important to the manager because of their role in the change process; of all the factors with which a manager deals, tasks are among the easiest to change. Also, they are decisive in modifying the nature of the organization. As a part of situational analysis it has been emphasized that one of the prime responsibilities of leadership is to make the organization adaptive to both external and internal conditions. If an organization is unable to adapt, it falls behind other evolving systems and becomes tied to the past. Making the organization responsive to change is, then, one of the key skills of leadership, but generating change is a very complex and difficult process.

Much of our management training has been directed at changing the people factor. Sensitivity training, training in management concepts, and many other forms of management development are directed at modifying the behavior and attitudes of people in organizations. However, that has been found to be both very slow and uncertain of success. Mature individuals with well-developed work habits and attitudes change only slowly if their work environment remains the same. For that reason, it is becoming more common to attempt to change other factors in the work environment. That comes down to changing the task and structure factors. Although the purpose and technology factors also adjust, they do so for reasons that are not as subject to management control.

Even though tasks can be changed much more quickly than people, they too are subject to certain organizational rigidities. Union-management labor agreements establish task structures that can be changed only through labor-management bargaining. Other tasks are dependent on processes and can be altered only through expensive machine modifications. Even so, many tasks in organizations can be changed by management decision. As job enlargement studies tend to prove, that kind of change can be a powerful force in modifying human behavior and increasing worker satisfaction. If, therefore, a manager is attempting to change certain aspects of his organization, one of the first things he should do is analyze the tasks performed. Change through task modification is one of the swiftest and surest methods of change at his disposal.

THE DIMENSIONS OF TASKS

The dimensions used to represent the attributes of tasks are given in Figure 4. Fifteen different dimensions are proposed, and many of them are in current use by different groups and professions. The first seven are part of the system utilized by the Bureau of Employment Security of the Department of Labor to classify jobs in the United States. To those who might be somewhat skeptical of the scale concept as it relates to factors and their dimensions, it should be noted that, in the 1965 edition of the *Dictionary of Occupational Titles*,[7] the Bureau of Employment Security has classified 21,741 separate occupations known by 13,809 additional titles, or a total of 35,550 job titles. It has done so by evaluating different occupations and their dimensions and by utilizing scales or gradation differences similar to those of Figure 4. Each of the 35,550 titles is differentiated by separate ratings of the dimensions used to represent characteristics of the occupation.

The first three dimensions in the job classification system are concerned with three of the most important features of tasks: the degree to which the job involves working with people, things, and data. In each instance the Bureau of Employment Security utilizes a nine-level hierarchy of

Figure 4. **Task factor dimensions.**

DIMENSIONS	MEANS OF EVALUATION
Working with people	1 (low) ———————————————————— (high) 10
Working with things	1 (low) ———————————————————— (high) 10
Working with information (data)	1 (low) ———————————————————— (high) 10
Reasoning skills	1 (low) ———————————————————— (high) 10
Mathematical skills	1 (low) ———————————————————— (high) 10
Language skills	1 (low) ———————————————————— (high) 10
Physical demands	1 (low) ———————————————————— (high) 10
Repetition (standardization)	1 (low) ———————————————————— (high) 10
Specialization and differentiation	1 (little required) ————————————— (high) 10
Sequential interdependence (continuity)	1 (little required) ————————————— (high) 10
Time range (job cycle)	1 (short) ———————————————————— (long) 10
Autonomy (independence)	1 (little) ———————————————————— (high) 10
Throughput rate	1 (low volume) ————————————— (high volume) 10
Organizational nature of task	Describe: line, staff, operational, support, supervisory, etc.
Functional nature of task	Describe: marketing, production, engineering, research, maintenance, etc.

complexity to measure the intricate relation of those dimensions with specific occupations. For instance, in the data hierarchy an eight rating is the lowest level and shows no significant relationship. The three level involves compiling of data. The top level of complexity, the zero level, involves synthesizing data.

The next three task dimensions are reasoning, mathematical, and language skills. Tasks are differentiated by the types of skills required to perform them. The reasoning, mathematical, and language dimensions are used in the *Dictionary of Occupational Titles* classification system to measure the general educational development required of a person to perform in an occupation effectively. Levels from a low of one to a high of six represent the complexity of a dimension as it relates to each occupation. For example, mathematical skills rated one would involve the performing of simple arithmetic as a part of the occupation and a six level would involve the application of advanced mathematical and statistical techniques.

All 35,550 occupational titles are also rated by the physical aspects of the job: the physical requirements of the occupation and the physical capacities a worker must have to meet them. Strength requirements are established by a five-point gradation, with sedentary work as the lowest and very heavy work as the highest. The latter involves lifting objects in excess of 100 pounds. Physical demands are among the features of production-type work, and for that reason appropriate dimensions are included in the situational model.

The next two dimensions listed in Figure 4 are among the most important in identifying the characteristics of tasks: they are the amount of repetition in the task and the degree to which the task is specialized. Highly repetitive tasks tend to be monotonous and psychologically unfulfilling for the worker. Production tasks that are highly specialized also tend to be routine and to encompass such a narrow range of activity that it is difficult for the worker to identify with the end product or with the objectives of the organization. The two dimensions are extremely important in the behavioral considerations of management. In a study by Hage and Aiken routine tasks were also found to correlate very positively with specific dimensions of organization structure. Organizations with routine tasks tend to have centralized decision making, a more formalized organization structure, and more specified jobs.[8]

The next four dimensions are some of the common differences among tasks. The sequential interdependence dimension has to do with the degree to which a series of tasks must be interrelated; the extreme example is an automotive assembly line. The time range dimension covers the total job cycle: the time range of assembling a radio is fairly short, whereas that of assembling a jet transport is long. Autonomy represents

71

the degree of independence in the tasks, one of the important motivational considerations. The throughput rate is a measure of the volume of a series of tasks. An operator of a machine stamping out 3,000 parts in an hour has a high throughput rate, whereas a worker engaged in the custom fabrication and machining of parts has a low throughput rate.

The last two dimensions are included because they are among the most common task designations in current use. The organizational activities in which people are engaged are represented by the nature of the tasks they perform.

Terms such as line, staff, support, and supervisory identify such activities; they have specific connotations in management literature and are therefore accepted means of designating the nature of tasks. That also applies to the functional designations of tasks. Such terms as marketing, production, finance, and engineering are commonly important to anyone who wants to describe what he does in an organization.

TECHNOLOGY AS AN INTERNAL FACTOR

Technology is considered as both an internal and an external factor of the firm. As an external factor, primary consideration is given to technology as a force for change in our society. As an internal factor, primary consideration is given to the status of the technology in a firm's operations and the conditions that level of technology creates through its impact on other internal factors. Ultimately the concern is for the implications of technology for managerial decision making.

Chapter 8 will deal with technology as an external factor; here we are concerned only with the importance of technology as a force that affects a firm and its internal operations. The history of industrialization and of changes that have occurred in business firms in this century supports an assertion that almost explosive advances have been powered to a significant degree by changes in technology. In fact, James D. Bright of the University of Texas, one of the leaders in the study of technological innovation, says that "technology is probably the most powerful force in today's business environment." [9] Unfortunately, it is also one of the least understood forces. The problems of assessing technology and of forecasting and evaluating the future influences of technology are just now receiving broad national attention. That is evidenced by the creation by Congress, in November 1972, of the Office of Technology Assessment.

The result is a dilemma for the management analyst. It is obvious that technology is one of the most intense forces for both external and internal change, but the exact nature of the force is uncertain. Cause-and-effect relationships cannot be specifically identified. Technology undoubtedly has a causal impact on other factors and on management systems, but there is also an interplay between those factors and systems. Without question, technology affects the structure of an organization, but specific structures can also be productive of certain technological changes. Accordingly, interrelationships are identified, but it is difficult to say whether they are dependent or only associative.

The Nature of Technology

In Chapter 3 technology is described as the tools, techniques, processes, and knowledge that extend human capability. It is a measure of the intellectual content of the tasks and machine operations performed by an organization. Technology represents the art of applying knowledge. Since much of that knowledge is now acquired by scientific investigation, technology is the bridge between science and industry. It is a measure of the level of knowledge represented by the machinery, the techniques required of the people who perform the operations, and the methodologies used in organizations. The measurement is in terms of the complexity or state of the art of the disciplines involved. If the knowledge utilized is derived from the frontiers of science, if it includes recent innovations, or if it represents the application of the most sophisticated concepts of a particular discipline, it is considered to represent a complexity consistent with the continuums utilized in measuring factors in the situational model. Simple technology usually involves little use of machinery, minimal expert knowledge, and a preponderance of routine, physical tasks.

A classification of industries and firms can be based on these differences; since all industries and firms are affected by technology, the differences are a matter of degree. However, industries with a high technological intensity would include aerospace, electronics, medical apparatus, and electronic data processing. Industries less affected by technology would be those with a higher service or labor input, as in restaurants, truck transportation, construction involving some crafts, and some government agencies, and industries in which technological updating is infrequent, as in some mining, refining, and processing enterprises. Small retail operations also are normally characterized by low technology.

The Significance of Technology

Technology deserves consideration by the manager and is a primary factor in the contingency model of management for the following five reasons:

1. Technology is a changing, dynamic force that generates changing, dynamic conditions in organizations that rely on technology in their operations.

2. Increases in the technology of a firm's operations are normally accompanied by managerial complexity. That is reflected in the complex

systems and concepts needed in the management of highly technological operations.

3. Technology is a major determinant of the people factor in an organization.

4. Technology, through its impact on people and tasks, has a major impact on organization structure.

5. The nature of the technology found in an organization and its operations tends to be one of the primary determinants of the type and nature of the planning, control, information, and business systems that will be effective in that organization.

Technology and Change

Technology is one of the primary factors in an organization because, as it changes, it tends to generate change in all other features of the organization. The rapid advance of technology in the operations peculiar to an industry forces the entire industry to experience change dynamics. Electronic data processing is a good example of rapid growth; the whole industry has mushroomed from the first scientific and business applications in the late 1940s. Aerospace is another spectacular example; the major product lines have tended to change every few years. The industry went from propeller-driven craft to jets and then to missiles, rockets, and space shuttles within 40 years. In contrast, many firms in the mining, processing, and transportation industries have not experienced major changes in their product lines for nearly 100 years, although they have been affected by the automation aspects of technology.

Change in an industry and within an organization has many influences on management. Change inevitably introduces some uncertainty, since the direction of change is not always easy to predict. Stability or lack of stability of operations tends to attract people with complementary temperaments. Change tends to generate opportunities, but it also generates insecurity, each of which affects the needs of the organization participants. One aerospace firm was surprised when all of the striking workers it had hired from a chemical industry returned to their former employer after a long strike ended. Those workers never did adjust to the instability of the aerospace firm.

When the technology of an organization changes, the people requirements change, the structure tends to change, the tasks being performed change, the needs of leadership change, and the systems needed to manage and control the operations frequently change. The major implication of a dynamic environment for managers is that the leadership role becomes oriented toward dealing with the change process. Adaptation to change consistent with the situational model of management becomes a prime responsibility of management. This involves more than anticipating change and maintaining an organization that is adaptive to change; it also involves keeping management techniques and systems developing at the pace of the technologies that they control.

Technology and Complexity

High-technology operations and processes tend to be extremely complex. Advanced technology is very esoteric and is bound up in technical sophistications that restrict thorough understanding of it to the high-level engineer or scientist. That complicates managerial understanding of many operations and processes and especially of the important process of communication. As a result it is difficult for many practitioners, such as accountants or computer programmers, to apply their art. The difficulty is in comprehending the operations to which their special skills are to be applied. Complexity in tasks and technology almost inevitably results in complex planning and control systems, complex decision making, and complex analysis of variables in a situation.

Advanced technology has also led to advance in the size of projects, another cause of increased complexity. The supersonic transport, the C-5A jet transport, and the 10-year $25 billion plus Apollo project are examples. Sheer size alone has pushed the financial requirements of the projects beyond the capacity of private industry, so that government involvement is becoming more common, as evidenced by the now-defunct supersonic transport, communication satellites, atomic energy reactors, and other similar projects. The government involvement itself contributes to the complexity of massive-engineering, high-technology programs.

The complexity of advanced technology has created many problems and headaches for management, but it has also created challenges that, by being met, have been responsible for some of the major management innovations since the early 1950s. Examples are network analysis techniques such as PERT, the program management organization concept developed as part of aerospace efforts, and advances in management information systems.

Technology and People

Technology is one of the major determinants of the nature of the work force in terms of the skills, knowledge, and temperament of the people involved. Engineering activities require engineers; metallurgical work requires metallurgists; R&D projects require scientific personnel. But technology also affects the nature of leadership. According to one of the propositions Stanley H. Udy, Jr. developed from his studies, "The greater the amount of technical knowledge required in an organization, the greater the emphasis on expertise as a basis of legitimate authority." [10] Increased technology places a premium on people with knowledge and skills related to the technology, and that applies to operations, staff, and leadership positions. As cautioned earlier, however, technology is not entirely an independent factor, nor is people entirely a dependent one. Leaders in power positions in organizations will select certain products or projects for a firm to work on because they involve technology consistent with their expertise and background.

Technology is normally related to machinery that extends human capability and hence to concepts of automation. As noted earlier, automation strongly influences people requirements. When firms introduce automation, machines take over the tasks once performed by people. Now the people required are those who regulate, maintain, and monitor the machinery. Those activities, of course, require skills significantly different from those formerly required to perform the tasks. If a firm decides to automate its warehousing operations, for example, the skills of the supervisor are no longer in knowing locations and in supervising subordinates who move items physically. Now supervisors must read computer printouts and be familiar with inventory problems associated with the mechanical conveying of the items.

Changes incident to automation have many effects on people, as terms such as retraining, feeling of achievement, insecurity, and status indicate. Automation is all too often undertaken with disregard for the social dislocation that it causes. In one actual warehousing example like that sketched in the preceding paragraph, over half of the first-line supervisors asked to be reduced to hourly employees because they felt they could not master the new skills associated with using computer printouts.

The diagram shows the relationship between technology and leadership styles. Scientists and others with unique expertise must for two reasons be

Advanced technology	→	People with technology skills	→	Permissive leadership styles

given a relatively free hand in utilizing their skills or knowledge. First, as indicated earlier, upper-level supervisors often know little of the scientists' areas of expertise, so that of necessity they must leave the scientists relatively free to make technical decisions. Second, professionals typically feel they should be governed by their professional codes, and they resent detailed control or autocratic leadership and do not function efficiently under it. Scientists typically have high self-actualization and recognition needs, and close supervision hinders them in satisfying those needs. Many of the studies already cited support that statement. Fiedler's studies show that research personnel call for relationship-oriented leadership. Udy and Perrow also support the proposition that unstructured, scientific tasks necessitate more unstructured, supportive-type supervision. The contingency approach to leadership styles will be covered in detail in Chapter 9.

Technology and Organization Structure

Changing, complex technology results in changing, complex organization structures. Advanced-technology organizations have been typified by frequent changes in structure and by a major reliance on temporary project groups and task forces to make them more adaptive. Warren Bennis has been a leader of the opinion that the turbulence of technology will force organizations of the future to be less structured. He expects them to be "adaptive, rapidly changing temporary systems." Such organizations will be structured "around problems-to-be-solved" and will be in a state of "organic flux." [11] He sees this temporary type of organization replacing the more structured, bureaucratic type of organization that now predominates.

Many of the research studies that have arisen from an attempt to relate types of tasks and technology have dealt with two different models of organization described as bureaucratic and organic. The bureaucratic organization is highly structured: jobs are precisely described; work methods are fully developed; and a large number of work rules and regulations dictate what is to be done. The organic organization has much less structure and thus is more flexible and adaptive. Most studies support the conclusion of the Walker and Lorsch study referred to earlier. Bureaucratic structure seems more appropriate in and efficient for routine production tasks, but organic structure is more necessary in operations that feature advanced technology and in which problem solving, not efficient production, is the primary issue.

In other studies Lawrence and Lorsch conclude, "We have seen strong indications that organizations with less formal structure and widely shared influence are best able to cope with uncertain and heterogeneous environmental conditions." [12] The impressive amount of research on this topic in recent years strongly supports the conclusion that organizations that feature different technologies function efficiently under different types of organization structure. Specific technologies tend to dictate certain types of structure, which is an extremely significant principle of situational analysis.

The impact of technology on organization structure is extremely pervasive. The Woodward studies, already referred to, relate spans of control, the number of levels in a hierarchy, and other such factors to different types of production technologies. The widespread use of the program management form of departmentation in the aerospace industry is a prime example of technology affecting structure. Essentially every major aerospace firm has converted from a functional or a process structure to a program structure since the early 1950s. An exploration of how technology has affected other aspects of organization structure such as job design would open up another whole avenue of investigation. Dependent relationships resulting from technology would undoubtedly be found.

Technology and Management Systems

The final reason why technology is an important management factor is that it tends to determine the types of planning, control, information, and business systems that will be successful in the management of specific operations. That will be dealt with in detail in Chapter 11, so only a brief summary will be included here.

High-technology programs, except those involving automation, are normally nonrepetitive ones referred to as one of a kind. They can be contrasted with the highly repetitive production involved in an automotive assembly line. The two different situations exert far different demands on management systems. Many of those system requirements have been recognized for years. Routine production involves known cost situations in which standard cost and flexible or variable budget systems can be utilized. High-technology projects, on the other hand, are pushing the frontiers of science, and cost experience is not available. Thus job order cost systems are utilized and a fixed-type budget system must normally be incorporated.

Planning and control systems have the same basis of variation. In routine, highly repetitive, production situations, the time to produce each unit is known and the production control problem is that of sequencing the items that go down the assembly line. That is known as flow control. In high-technology one-of-a-kind projects with many unknowns a broader range of factors must be estimated and tracked for accuracy. Management systems must take into consideration uncertainties that involve the sequencing of activities, the estimated time factors, performance criteria, and resource requirements. That calls for Gantt-chart techniques, such as milestone scheduling, or network analysis techniques, such as PERT. Note that PERT has no application to repetitive production; its only valid application is to relatively unknown or nonrepetitive situations.

Most other business systems are influenced by the technology of organizations. Situations that are relatively stable permit the development of particular types of systems, normally those that are highly detailed and directed at finite controls. Changing, complex situations that result from advanced technology involve systems that are normally less structured but also more tenuous because of the unknowns. If technology forces organizations to be more temporary in structure as Bennis predicts, that will have many implications for planning and control systems because most such systems are built around the authority structure of an organization.

TECHNOLOGY DIMENSIONS

The dimensions of the technology factor (Figure 5) are relatively few. Essentially, technology is measured by the technical content of the activities and processes of an organization. Accordingly the first three dimensions cover the technical content of methodologies, operations, and machinery. Besides those three dimensions, an important indicator is the amount of automation. Associated with automation is the complexity of the man–machine interface, the problem of integrating people and machines. These psychotechnology considerations are becoming more important to the manager.

Frequently, the physical effects that accompany technology are an important consideration. Certain technologies create heat problems, radiation hazards, noise pollution, or other discomforts or strains that must be recognized by supervision. A descriptive dimension is therefore included to cover those factors.

Figure 5. Technology factor dimensions.

DIMENSIONS	MEANS OF EVALUATION
Technical content of methodologies	1 (low) .... (high) 10
Technical content of operations	1 (low) .... (high) 10
Technical content of machinery	1 (low) .... (high) 10
Automation	1 (little) .... (high) 10
Man–machine interface	1 (simple) .... (complex) 10
Physical effects	Describe: heat, sound, eyestrain, muscular strain, etc.
Methodology and function	Describe: production (unit, batch, continuous process), research (basic, applied), etc.

The final dimension of technology is traditional nomenclature, descriptive terms that define the complexity of different types of functions. They are not shown as continuums because for a complete listing hundreds would be involved. The standard example is the one used in the Woodward studies, in which production was divided into unit, batch, and continuous process methodologies. As another example, in research the traditional designation has been basic or pure versus applied.

Two of the most important factors that affect management conditions are task and technology, yet very little research has been devoted to them and their significance. Instead, attention has tended to focus on behavioral considerations in motivation, different leadership styles, concepts of formal organization structure, and planning and control methodologies. The task and technology factors deserve much more attention in management literature. They must be properly diagnosed and interpreted before formal organization principles, planning and control systems, or other concepts of management can be successfully applied.

seven
organization structure as a factor

THE MOST IMPORTANT institutions affecting individuals and society at large are organizations. Essentially, all human behavior is conducted within the constraints of organizational life and all monumental achievements are the product of group effort. During most of his life the individual is connected with various formal organizations and carries on his activities as a part of them. Political, social, and economic power are essentially the domain of organizations, and individuals normally have significant power only through their operating or leadership positions in organizations. In our pluralistic society, organizations are the great instruments of effectiveness, and it is through them that individuals have influence. Anyone who works alone has little economic or political impact; by working through organizations, he can have potential for both that is tremendous.

The importance of organizations has long since been reflected in management theory, which is most fully developed in regard to organization structure. Books on general management have tended to overconcentrate on formal organization concepts simply because a vast amount of information is available. Initially comprehensive lists of formal organization principles were developed, and in more recent years they have been supplemented by detailed theories about the informal aspects of organizations.

Most formal concepts of organization are familiar to the reader and will not be dealt with in detail, but several comments on the development of organizational concepts are appropriate. Usually the approaches were too atomistic; only one aspect of an organization was viewed or the problems of, say, internal structure were dealt with rather than those of the organization as a whole. Also, not enough consideration was given to organization structure as it is related to other important factors, especially tasks, technology, people, and the external environment.

Accordingly, this analysis will focus on relationships among the major factors and their effect on organization structure. As has already been indicated, technology and tasks tend to be leading variables in terms of their influence on structure. If an organization is to be effective, it must be consistent with the demands of tasks, technology, and the external environment. Being an effective organizer thus requires a broad perspective, much broader than mere acquaintance with a listing of formal organization concepts.

DEFINITION OF STRUCTURE

The distinction between an organization and organization structure is significant. In the broad sense an organization includes people, resources, and all the policies, regulations, methods, codes of conduct, tasks, and other activities or guidelines that govern the utilization and relationships of people and resources. Each contributes to the image that an organization develops. Formal structure, on the other hand, is essentially restricted to the system of relationships deliberately established by those in authority. It results from the process of grouping tasks and activities into positions and establishing relationships among those positions to achieve certain goals and objectives.

The key point is that formal organization structure consists of the established positions and the relationships among them, not of people and their relationships. To establish a position designated as purchasing agent under the vice-president of administration is an act of formal organization. To assign John as purchasing agent is referred to as a staffing function. Informal structure comes into existence when John assumes the position of purchasing agent and, through social interaction, develops certain relationships with the vice-president of administration and with other individuals and groups in the organization. The informal organization structure that evolves from interpersonal relations is frequently as important as or more important than the formal structure.

Organization structure, then, is a system of relationships, formally prescribed and informally developed, that govern the activities of people who are dependent upon each other for the accomplishment of common goals or the satisfaction of common needs. In a formal structure, positions are prescribed to designate specific associated tasks and responsibilities. Relationships among the positions are also defined to the end of maximizing the synergy effect of group effort. The informal structure reflects the actual functioning of the organization when people have assumed the positions and modified, confirmed, and/or expanded the formal relationships through the process of social interaction. Formal organization is how those in authority want an organization to function; informal organization is how it actually functions.

In behavioral science literature organizations are commonly defined as systems of roles. Since organizations are essentially comprised of individuals, the organization analyst is concerned with what governs human behavior in group activity. Basically, that has been shown to be the role assumed by the individual when he accepts membership in an organization. The role consists of behavior patterns expected of him in his specific position. The expectations are both formally and informally developed. The position descriptions, procedures, and other formal trappings represent the expectations of management, whereas informal expectations have no advance expression—they are developed through association and interaction with other individuals. And although those individuals are both inside and outside the organization, the most important informal expectations are those of immediate subordinates, supervisors, peers, and other associates.

According to both managerial and behavioral definitions, structure is a system of relationships. Managerial definitions place more emphasis on authority relationships, grouping of tasks, and integration of activities. Behavioral definitions concentrate on how the expectations of others influence behavior. As so often happens, the management writer is interested in prescribing what should be done and the behavioralist in describing what is done.

IMPORTANCE OF STRUCTURE

There are six reasons why structure is a significant factor in management and one of the primary concerns of supervision:

Structure represents the functional and authority relationships that govern the work flow of the organization. The manner in which those relationships are established influences the effectiveness of resource utilization. Establishing formal structure is the means by which the work is divided up, responsibility for decision making is established, and control procedures are instituted.

Through structure, management can focus on the key activities of the organization, because the structure is established to highlight the essential organization functions. A retail organization will feature its selling activities; a production organization will insure that the production functions predominate. From a systems standpoint boundaries are established and relationships that control the functioning of the organization are designated.

The structure of an organization is the framework through which the management systems flow. Planning, control, information, and business systems all normally follow the functional and authority relationships established as a part of the structure. If the structure is ill-conceived, the operation of those systems and managerial decision making are hindered.

As indicated earlier, the manner in which tasks are structured and authority to perform those tasks is delegated is a prime determinant of motivation in an organization. Since organizations are established to achieve specific goals through people, the structuring of activities to encourage individual and group productivity is very important.

The authority to modify organization structure is one of the most important potential controls of management. Situational theory holds that one of the primary responsibilities of the manager is to maintain an adaptive organization. Changing the organization structure or maintaining a flexible structure is a fundamental mechanism of the adaptation process, and it is one of the primary ways of encouraging change that the manager has. As indicated earlier, individual behavior is highly resistant to change unless environmental changes, such as manipulating formal structure, are undertaken as well. However, changing organization structure does not automatically modify behavior. Human behavior patterns are often deeply ingrained and defense mechanisms are highly effective, so that mere changes in titles or position descriptions result in only a slight modification of what is done. Changing the formal structure is complex because it involves not merely a reshuffling of formal relationships but also a tampering with the social structure, which has many behavioral implications.

The formal structure of an organization helps determine social relationships and patterns of social interaction. Positioning of workers along fixed work stations determines who is physically available for social interaction. Formal positions and delegated authority also affect the status relationships that are established. Because formal structure influences the social system, it is an important factor in the evolution of the organization subculture.

DIMENSIONS OF STRUCTURE

A large number of principles of formal organization have been developed, and so it is necessary to be selective in identifying the primary dimensions of structure to avoid a list that is prohibitively long and complex. Fourteen dimensions are given in Figure 6, but many of them, such as informal structure, actually represent a group of dimensions. The dimensions of primary concern in a particular situation would be further elaborated. The dimensions selected for Figure 6 are those that have been given greatest attention in management literature and those that are typically involved in the structuring of group activity.

The Scale Dimension

One of the most important dimensions of structure in respect to a manager's activities is the size of the organization. Size will influence the following factors: consistency in the amount of authority delegated, levels in the hierarchy, staff services available, methods of communication, and the formalization of business systems. In smaller organizations there are typically fewer levels in the hierarchy, less delegation of authority, fewer staff services, a reliance on verbal communication, and a shortage of formalized business systems. Large organizations tend to be more bureaucratic. As Udy concludes from his studies, "The larger the size of the organization, . . . the greater the over-all emphasis on formal and impersonal rules and specificity of roles." [1]

Size also tends to complicate management. There are more elements

Figure 6. **Structure factor dimensions.**

DIMENSIONS	MEANS OF EVALUATION	
Scale (size)	1 (few employees)	(many) 25,000
Hierarchy	1 (few levels)	(many) 15
Authority delegation	1 (decentralized)	(centralized) 10
Span of control	1 (few subordinates)	(many subordinates) 40
Integration of activities	1 (low requirement)	(high requirement) 10
Geographical dispersion	1 (one location)	(many locations) 20
Job specifications	1 (general)	(very detailed) 10
Formalization	1 (few rules and procedures)	(many rules 10 and procedures)
Nature of authority	Describe: line, staff, functional, concurring, etc.	
Departmentation	Type: functional, program, territorial, process, customer.	
Special structures	Classify and describe: service, staff, committee, task force, etc.	
Openness of membership	1 (few barriers)	(many barriers) 10
Group cohesiveness	1 (low)	(high) 10
Informal structure	Describe the nature of social structure including roles, communication channels, group norms, power structure, and patterns of interaction.	

to coordinate, more individuals to inform, and frequently less employee identification with overall purpose and objectives. In large organizations subgroups tend to put their own interests first, and this results in suboptimal decision making. Also, human relations are not as satisfying. People tend to work more effectively in small groups of six to eight in which they can come to know each other better and feel more secure in their social relationships.

The ramifications of the size of an organization are many. By itself size is not overpowering in creating managerial complexity, but when it is combined with other variables, especially sophisticated technology, it tends to strain our existing knowledge of management. Firms such as Lockheed Aircraft and Douglas Aircraft demonstrated the truth of that statement in the late 1960s.

Size can also influence management strategy. One of the characteristics of most organizations is a propensity to grow. Growth is, in fact, often considered a measure of success, even of survival. As firms grow in size, they tend to seek new markets, new product lines, or new functions. Managers are under pressure to keep their manpower, equipment, facilities, and financial resources fully utilized. To do so, they are constantly searching for new opportunities and expansion of current operations. The strong commitment to operate at full capacity supported by a large backlog of orders often results in an almost irrational surge toward expansion. Size and growth force many adjustments in management and thus have a strong dependent effect on other variables.

Dimensions and Authority Relationships

Three dimensions have to do with authority relationships: the number of levels in the hierarchy, the authority delegated, and the span of control. In turn, the number of levels in the hierarchy is closely related to size: normally, the larger the organization the more numerous the levels. But hierarchy is also associated with authority delegation and decentralization. Flat organizations that feature few levels require broader delegation of authority. Sears Roebuck is an example of a major corporation that has attempted to develop a flat organization in order to improve communication within its structure and encourage greater delegation of authority.

A large number of levels in a hierarchy normally means greater complexity. Referring decisions through numerous channels typically slows down the decision-making process. Also, communication becomes more difficult. Every time communication passes through a channel, it experiences some distortion.

The number of levels in a hierarchy affects the superior-subordinate ratio; the fewer the levels, the larger the ratio. That has important financial implications, since supervision is a major part of overhead cost.

As a dependent variable, hierarchy is affected by the size and age of the organization, degree of organization specialization, the type of ownership (family or corporate), and other such factors. In its turn, hierarchy affects the amount of decentralization, the speed and accuracy of decision making, the effectiveness of communication, the morale of subordinates, unit costs, and productivity.

Centralization and Decentralization

Centralization versus decentralization resulting from authority delegation was the subject of Chapter 4. Eleven dimensions were established as the primary ones that affect decisions on decentralization. It was noted that centralization encourages coordination and conformity, reduces duplication, increases central control, improves decision making by broadening the perspective, avoids suboptimization, permits use of staff experts, and satisfies the ego needs and power demands of leadership. Decentralization tends to reduce the top-executive work load, is highly motivational for lower-level employees because of the freedom it affords, results in more productivity, helps develop managers, encourages quicker decisions, permits consideration of local conditions in decision making, and makes possible the establishment of competitive parallel organizational units.

Span of Control

Span of control is closely associated with the number of levels in a hierarchy; it deals with the number of subordinates who report directly to a supervisor. If the number of levels is reduced, the span of control must be increased because there are the same number of people but fewer subgroups. Six significant variables affect the span of control:

The skills, attitudes, and training of people. The more capable people are, the less direction they require and the broader the appropriate span.

The routine, repetitive nature of the tasks performed. Routine tasks can be mastered in a short period of time, and little training or follow-up direction is required.

The complexity of the technology associated with the tasks. If the tasks involve technical complexity, the supervisor needs more time to comprehend and monitor what is taking place, and the result is a narrower span of control.

The differentiation and autonomy of the tasks. Highly specialized tasks usually require more supervision if each subordinate is engaged in different duties. Autonomous tasks such as selling normally involve less supervisory time.

Formalization of the structure. Organizations with a large number of rules, regulations, policies, and procedures governing the work performed require more supervision time for enforcement and control purposes.

Interfaces with other organizations. The more the work of a unit relates to the work of other units with high sequential interdependence, the more supervision time is required to coordinate those relationships.

The favorable results of a small span of control are as follows: Much better control and direction are generally achieved owing to the low ratio of subordinates per supervisor. The supervisor has more time to interact with individual subordinates, and so he understands them better. Low spans result in small groups that are normally more cohesive and have better employee identification and social interaction. Finally, small groups considerably ease the communication problem.

Large spans of control are normally associated with the following favorable effects: The cost of supervision is lower because of the higher supervisor-subordinate ratio. Subordinates have more independence because a supervisor does not have time for individual direction of those reporting to him. The result is a flatter organization that is normally more motivational for low-level employees because of the greater freedom of operation. Finally, a large span of control improves vertical communication and decision making because there are fewer levels in the organization.

Integration and Dispersion of Activities

The degree to which the activities of an organization are integrated and the dispersion of the activities in an organization are two important features of structure. Lawrence and Lorsch have identified integration as one of the most important characteristics of organizations. Integration involves the unity of effort among the subunits or subsystems of an organization. It represents the degree of collaboration within an organization.

The need for integration is strongly affected by the tasks and products of the organization and by pressures from the external environment. Diverse tasks and diverse products result in a need for integration. Varied, conflicting, subgroup goals and conflict in interpersonal relations also result in a need for integration. In addition, competitive conditions in the marketplace of a firm, including the rapidity of technological change, affect a firm's reliance on integration.

The benefits of integration are improved coordination, quick response, and a more adaptive organization. As organizations become larger in size and as conglomerates and multinational corporations become increasingly common, integrative features of organizations become more critical to success. Means of integration include committees, task forces, and

89

special organizational units such as the matrix form of program management.

Geographical dispersion is primarily a function of the organization's tasks and purposes. Post offices, chain stores, and sales offices must be dispersed to meet the needs of their clientele. Distribution is also affected by size; many manufacturing firms have concluded that administrative efficiency decreases when plant size goes beyond 10,000 employees. Environmental considerations also tend to force distribution. For example, the garment and textile industry experienced significant migration from the northeastern to the southern states, where a workforce at lower pay scales was readily available.

As indicated earlier, geographically dispersed plants tend to be decentralized and to enjoy the special advantages of profit decentralization. On the other hand, widely distributed plants tend to lose the advantages of centralization. Dispersed plants are easier to administer as separate entities, but they present problems in overall company conformity, integration, and coordination.

Formality of Organization Structure

Two dimensions have to do with the formalization of the organization structure; they are the job specifications, which cover the positions in the organization, and the formalization of the structure as represented by the rules and procedures that govern broader organizational relationships. The degree to which job descriptions and specifications are detailed depends to a significant degree on the continuity of operations and the size of the organization. When the work flow is continuous and the structure is large, positions and job specifications tend to be precisely described. When work is nonrepetitive and the activities of the organization are frequently changing, job descriptions are more general. In smaller organizations, in which people are required to perform a variety of tasks, job descriptions are found less frequently and, when they do exist, are less detailed.

Detailed job descriptions are an aid in communicating the requirements of a job and in pinpointing responsibilities and controls. They are also essential in the matching of skills with job demands. The dangers of excessively detailed job descriptions is that they tend to hem people in and discourage creativity and innovation. They also tend to be inflexible and consequently to contribute to the rigidity of the organization.

The formalization dimension in Figure 6 represents the procedures, policies, rules, and regulations that specify what is to be done in an organization. Highly formalized companies have a large number of organization and procedural manuals that dictate activity steps and responsibilities. As indicated earlier, organizations are usually highly formalized when tasks are routine and repetitive. Not only does the routine nature of the tasks permit such formalization but the lack of natural motivators in such tasks makes it necessary to control the work being performed.

Among other factors that affect formalization are purpose and ownership. Government agencies are normally more formalized because of their need to be accountable to the public and because of the ancient distrust of public servants. Age of an organization is also a factor. New requirements and situations generate new procedures, but, like the laws of government, few of the old procedures are ever discarded.

The final factor in formalization is the nature of leadership. If leaders have confidence in and trust their subordinates, they are not as apt to tie them down with rules and regulations. Leaders who distrust their subordinates are apt to have a passion for extensive rules and regulations.

The advantages of formalization are the advantages of bureaucracy: formalization makes operations more predictable, consistent, and orderly. However, those virtues are offset by the rigidities and feelings of distrust built into the organization. Operations that are overproceduralized are cumbersome, slow to react, and difficult to change. The reward systems tend to discourage innovation and compensate the conformist. As the environment of organizations has become more dynamic, the demands of adaptation have brought into question the efficiency advantages of bureaucratic organizations.

TRADITIONAL DIMENSIONS OF STRUCTURE

Three structure dimensions are included in Figure 6 to represent the most common traditional means of classifying organizations and internal authority relationships. The first dimension classifies the nature of authority by using the familiar line-staff designations. The second dimension covers different forms of departmentation, and the third encompasses special structures such as service groups, committees, and task forces.

Even though line and staff designations have been used to define authority relationships in religious and military organizations for centuries, confusion still surrounds their meaning. For that reason and also because of the claim that they do not fit reality, many have argued that the terms are obsolete and should be replaced. They are, however, still the most common way to describe authority relationships. Line authority is exercised by those who have direct responsibility for accomplishing the organization's objectives. It is broad authority delegated from the top: executives authorize subordinates to take action and command others in activities that directly advance the interests of the enterprise.

91

Basically, staff authority is not authority at all; instead it is a relationship to line positions and organizations such that staff groups or individuals serve only in an advisory capacity. In theory, staff positions are support elements that assist line organizations in accomplishing the goals of the enterprise. Here enters one of the confusing aspects of the line-staff authority concept: Which individuals and organizations contribute directly and which indirectly to accomplishing the goals? The distinctions are often unclear, and hence the answers are often quite arbitrary. However, it is important for an individual who is functioning in either capacity to know what authority he has in relation to other individuals and other groups.

Line-staff concepts have been confused in other ways in modern times. Originally, the decision makers and the people with power in organizations were the line executives. However, as staff groups have tended to proliferate and as major functions such as planning have been drawn away from line organizations and assigned to staff groups, more of the power in giant corporations resides in staff organizations.

Functional and concurring authority are normally associated with staff groups. Functional authority is the right to command others in regard to a function assigned to an organization—the budget director, for example, can prescribe the budget formats to be used. Functional authority does not normally overlap or invade any of the line end-product areas of authority. The typical example of concurring authority is the requirement that a staff group must concur in a decision made by a line organization—the personnel department, for example, must approve a salary offer to an engineer.

Departmentation as a Dimension

Five terms are traditionally used to classify departmentation: functional, program, territorial, process, and customer. Functional departmentation is still the most common type. The organization is subdivided on the basis of skill specializations, so that engineers, accountants, and quality control specialists are grouped into separate units. Program organizations are structured around product lines or major projects. Territorial, process, and customer organizations are self-explanatory.

Like the line and staff designations, traditional departmentation terms have been criticized in recent years. They are said to be primarily descriptive titles with little prescriptive value. Some groups, primarily sociologists, have looked for better ways to differentiate organization types. It is becoming popular to consider subgroups as subsystems and to classify them on the basis of their function: production, support, maintenance, adaptation, or management.

It is true that the traditional departmentation classifications do not cover all types of subgroups within an organization. Accordingly, a dimension entitled special structures is included in Figure 6 to cover service groups, staff groups, committees, task forces, and other organizational elements that are coming into common use but do not fit the other dimensions.

SOCIAL DIMENSIONS OF ORGANIZATIONS

The last three dimensions of structure relate primarily to the informal aspects of organizations: openness of membership, group cohesion, and informal structure. Openness of membership has to do with both formal and informal barriers. Formal barriers include closed shop union agreements, such job specifications as skill levels, years of experience, and education, licenses, and apprenticeships. They and other restrictions on hiring serve as major filters to organization membership. Informal barriers include the attitudes of the current membership, role concepts, status relationships, restricted social interaction, and informal criteria used to constrain or expand associations.

The cohesiveness of a work group has many implications for the manager and is an important social dimension of the structure. A cohesive group that is committed to organizational objectives greatly reduces the burdens of supervision. The group itself tends to discipline its members, and it willingly cooperates in furthering the interests of the organization. On the other hand, a cohesive group that does not accept the goals of the organization presents one of management's most difficult problems. The strength of the group normally exceeds the power of the supervisor, who is put in a position of having to win group support if he is to attain his objectives. Still, groups that lack cohesion are characterized by more conflict and are less willing to cooperate. Therefore, they are much more difficult to manage.

Group cohesion is frequently a function of the degree to which individual needs are satisfied through the achievement of group goals. It is also affected by the compatibility of interpersonal relations, the existence of external threats to the group, the extent of individual involvement in decision making regarding group activities, and the homogeneity of the value systems and norms of group members.

The last dimension of structure concerns the characteristics of informal organization; they include established roles, patterns of interaction, communication channels, group norms, status relationships, and other features that characterize the behavior of people in any kind of group. Each group is unique in respect to each of those characteristics, and each characteristic could itself be a separate dimension of structure. It is not for several reasons. The list of dimensions in Figure 6 is already long, and any extension would confuse rather than clarify. Also, behavioralists are inclined to view the characteristics as processes rather than structure. Since organizational behavior is in a constant state of change in respect to the characteristics, the structure concept is rejected as implying both stability and unchanging parts. The formal aspects of structure such as delegation of authority and span of control are dimensions that the manager can change, whereas informal group processes are normally beyond his direct control.

However, that does not imply that the manager has no need to be familiar with informal aspects of organizations. As indicated earlier, informal organization is frequently as important as formal structure in determining group activity, productivity, and individual behavior. Accordingly, a manager must be aware of informal group dimensions if he is to apply his managerial skills appropriately. The degree to which particular concepts or techniques of management will be effective is frequently determined by informal organization.

STRUCTURE AND SITUATIONAL METHODOLOGY

In the situational methodology view of structure, the problem of organization involves an analysis of the factors that will affect the functioning of a particular structure. A manager does not apply principles of organization in a vacuum; instead he assumes particular tasks and activities are to take place and involve particular people with particular skills. His aim is to integrate those factors and achieve the goals of the organization. He thus needs to consider the key characteristics or the dimensions of the factors he is working with. The structure he selects must fit the tasks to be undertaken—the people who will be engaged in them and their technical complexity—if he is to achieve the goals he desires.

The manager also needs to be aware of the forces in the environment that enhance or constrain what he intends to accomplish. If he produces products to sell to the government, he must be concerned with how his structure will interface with government agencies. If he is to attract labor and other resources to his organization, he must develop a structure that is appealing to individuals, investors, and community groups. If his product involves manufacturing processes that discharge pollutants, he must be concerned with how his organization will interact with governmental and community organizations.

Two examples of decision making regarding structure will be used to illustrate situational analysis. If a manager is pondering the span of control appropriate to his organization, he will find it determined to a significant degree by the nature of the tasks. If the tasks are routine, repetitive, and uniform among group members, the span of control could be very large, perhaps as high as 25 or 30 to 1. Under those conditions the supervisor needs to spend little time in training the individuals in what is to be done or in the technical aspects of the task. His concerns are the general scheduling of the work and the people problems related to absenteeism, morale, and conflict situations. On the other hand, if a manager is the head of a task force in which each individual is performing a different set of complicated tasks, a span of control ratio of 6 to 1 might be appropriate. The leader of a task force must spend considerable time in coordinating and integrating diverse tasks if the group is to be effective.

If a company is going to build a new plant and is trying to decide on its size, many dimensions regarding structure must be considered. What economies of scale come from more massive production? What tasks and series of tasks must be performed to provide the completed product or service? What is the availability of labor? What communication problems arise from the tasks and technology? What staff services are needed? Do the tasks and technology result in administrative complexity? Should the psychological climate of the plant be conducive to conformity or to innovation? What services are available in the area?

Other detailed examples of decentralization and formalization have already been given. In each instance sound decisions on structure could be made only after a consideration of other leading factors such as task and technology.

Supporting Studies

Many recent studies support the situational approach to management structure. Those of Lawrence and Lorsch are prime examples; they indicate that there is no one best approach. Organizations engaged in highly standardized, predictive tasks perform better with structures characterized by highly formalized procedures and management hierarchies. Firms with more uncertain tasks that involve problem solving function best with less formalization and a greater emphasis on self-control and wide participation in decision making. Lawrence and Lorsch concluded that appropriate patterns of organization are contingent on the nature of the work to be done and on the needs of the people involved.

In an interesting study that was an extension of the Lawrence and Lorsch research efforts, John J. Morse worked with Lorsch in a survey of four organizations, two of which involved standardized production and the other two R&D operations.[2] They concluded that, to be successful, organization structure must fit the variables in a situation, primarily task and people. They state that "one important implication of the Contingency Theory is that we must not only seek a fit between organization and task, but also between task and people and between people and organization." They also concluded, "Although this inter-relationship is complex, the best possibility for managerial action probably is in tailoring the organization to fit the task and the people. If such a fit is achieved, both effective unit performance and a higher sense of competence motivation seem to result." [3]

SITUATIONAL AND TRADITIONAL APPROACHES TO STRUCTURE

An examination of the structure factor in situational analysis is not complete without an explanation of how the contingency approach differs from the traditional, bureaucratic approach to structure. The early writers on management theory, such as Henri Fayol, James D. Mooney, Allan C. Reiley, Luther Gulick, and Lyndall F. Urwick, dealt mostly with structural anatomy. They attempted to develop principles that could be applied to all organizations. Those principles have been widely accepted by practitioners, and many of them are included as dimensions of structure in Figure 6. They comprise important management knowledge even though recent research findings and theoretical developments indicate their limitations.

Classical theory focuses almost entirely on formal structure; it emphasizes the importance of the hierarchy, often referred to as the scalar chain. Through departmentation, functions are grouped in vertical fashion. Authority is then delegated from the top down through the chain of command that comprises the hierarchy. The hierarchy is the conduit through which communication, direction, and business systems are to flow.

Once a hierarchy is established, the problem becomes that of developing control and maintaining order within it. The solution is to apply the principle of unity of command and keep the span of control small enough so a supervisor can direct and monitor essentially everything that goes on within his part of the organization. Procedures and regulations are written to establish duties and responsibilities. They further structure and order the activities of the organization.

Once the basic structure is established, the next question is that of efficiency: how can workers be organized to maximize it? The traditional answer has been to make tasks simple, clearly defined, consistent, and highly specialized. Precisely defined, routine tasks are said to make work easy to master and to promote productivity. Getting people to work hard is considered to be a two-pronged problem. The supervisor should be given sufficient authority to force people to work, and economic incentives should be provided to entice them to work. The primary reliance on authority results in detailed distinctions of authority relationships relating to line and staff concepts, centralization and decentralization, accountability, and functional responsibilities. Emphasis is placed on formal statements that specify functions and authority delegations formalized by position descriptions and organizational manuals.

In the classical approach the emphasis is on utilizing reason and logic to piece together a structure that will order everything formally done in an organization in such a way that the organization will function automatically. If an organization structure is clear and precise, it should be obvious to people what is to be done and to whom they should look for direction.

Limitations of Traditional Approaches

Criticisms of the content of classical organization principles can be divided into five groups. They should really be viewed more as limitations than criticisms, since writers and practitioners alike generally accept the principles as important even while arguing that they are rapidly being outmoded. The limitations, then, of the classical principles are as follows:

First, they are inadequate because they are too simple and limited to reflect the total structure and functioning of an organization; they represent only one aspect of organization structure. Essentially, they ignore informal organization and the effect of human relations on group behavior. Some critics argue that classical writers left people out of organizations; they covered the way in which work should be divided and authorized, but they neglected the man doing the job. In traditional theory the motivational assumptions are too simplified; they are that people automatically respond to authority and economic rewards. The needs people have for self-actualization, recognition, acceptance, and security are essentially ignored. Man is perceived in a limited economic framework rather than a broader socioeconomic one.

The leadership assumption, also oversimplified, is that leadership is derived almost solely from authority. That ignores leadership styles and knowledge, the ability to satisfy needs, personal qualities, and other factors in group acceptance of a supervisor. Also, in classical theory there is little reference to decision-making processes in groups and to conflict within groups. The concepts of formal organization are important, but they account for only one aspect of the functioning of organizations.

The second criticism of traditional principles is that they are too broad and general to be meaningful. That limitation stems from the universalist assumption underlying the principles. Ernest Dale states that "a principle broad enough to cover all types of situations is necessarily so broad as to tell us little we did not know before." [4] Basically, classical theorists assumed that managerial functions in various types of organizations have common features and can therefore be included in concepts that have universal validity. The component principles are to be applied regardless of the differences in people, tasks, technology, or purpose. That, of course, is the point at which situational analysis is in most direct conflict with the traditional approach.

A third limitation of traditional concepts is associated with the goal of establishing a structure that is specific, exact, detailed, and predictable. To classical theorists the organization is best thought of as a fixed hierarchy. That is in sharp contrast with the view of behavioralists, to whom an organization is a social process, not something fixed. Organization structure consists of a system of relationships, some of which are dictated by managers at the top but many of which are developed through the social interaction of the organization members. In one view the structure is static and rigid; in the other it is dynamic and adaptive. For those reasons the term "mechanistic" has been used to describe traditional approaches and "organic" to describe behavioral approaches.

Traditional theorists also ignored the dynamic input-output model of systems theory. To systems theorists, on the other hand, organization structures are not rigid. To them, a structure is a series of flows and processes beginning with inputs of energy, materials, and information from the environment and ending with outputs of goods and services to organizations and systems in the environment.

There is no question that organizations do exhibit structure. Spans of control exist; restrictions are put on membership; formal functions are grouped in certain ways; and informal groups develop patterns of interpersonal relations that tend to be repeated. However, there are also constant internal and external forces and interactions that affect those relationships and cause them to change. Understanding and effectively reacting to those variables is the problem confronting the situational analyst.

A fourth criticism of traditional organizational principles is that they concentrate on internal structure. Hierarchy, span of control, and related principles establish a structure that maximizes internal efficiency and control. The problem of being responsive to outside forces is ignored. Concentration on internal order and precision in operations gears management to an overconcern with what goes on inside an organization and an underemphasis on external changes dealing with markets, competitors, technologies, and governments. Again, it is the recurring problem of adaptation.

98

The fifth criticism of formal organization principles is that they are directed at obtaining known, predictable behavior; people are expected to conform to rules, regulations, and procedures and to fit position descriptions closely. The principles are also based on an assumption of highly specialized, routine tasks. Such principles are inconsistent with the independence and achievement needs of people. In the bureaucratic environment a worker tends to be rewarded for conforming to rules, production standards, and dictates of supervision rather than for challenging current methods and processes, developing innovative approaches, and personalizing his job in the sense of matching his skills to its requirements. In conformist environments individuals are not encouraged to be creative. Overspecialization into highly routine tasks drains jobs of most of their psychological satisfaction.

Situational Approaches

The five limitations of classical theory comprise the major differences between traditional and situational approaches to organization structure. Situational theory holds that the principles of organization do not prescribe any specific structure; instead they are guidelines available to the manager after he has analyzed the factors in his particular situation. Organizations are considered not as static structures but as constantly changing entities that, if successfully managed, adapt to internal and external forces. Structure consists of a set of relationships that must be properly molded to the tasks, technology, and people of an organization and to external institutions and forces.

eight
environmental factors

A CENTRAL THESIS of situational analysis is that one of management's primary responsibilities is to adapt the organization to an ever-changing environment. That adaptation is essential if the firm is to continue to meet the needs of society and prosper as an organization. To illustrate the interplay between organization and environment, two closely related examples will be considered.

ENVIRONMENTAL FACTORS IN PLANT LOCATION

A major analytical task that confronts the management of an industrial firm is to select a plant site for the initiation or expansion of activities. Plant location decisions are typically based on a study by a group of specialists in plant location or by an ad hoc task force of individuals who represent various technical specialties or operating functions of the firm. Normally a checklist of factors important in plant location is established. The factors are weighted by their importance in the functioning of the plant. A typical list of plant location factors is the following:

1. Labor considerations:
   Availability of labor supply
   Types of skills available
   Wage rates in the region
   Productivity of the labor
   Extent of unionism
   Existence of right-to-work laws
2. Support services:
   Energy sources (electricity, oil, natural gas, fuels, etc.)
   Transportation (rail, air, truck, and water)
   Communication systems
   Financial services (banks, investment firms, etc.)
   Skilled subcontractors (construction, machining, research, etc.)
   Water supply—amount and cost
   Sewage disposal
   Insurance
3. Market locations:
   Proximity to raw materials
   Proximity to subcontractors and suppliers of components
   Proximity to customers
   Types of existing industries in the area
4. Tax structure:
   Property tax rates
   State income, sales, and other taxes
   Community taxes
   Existence of free-port laws

5. Land:
   Prices
   Availability
   Opportunities for future expansion
6. Climate:
   Rainfall
   Humidity
   Temperature extremes
   Unusual conditions (fog, hurricanes, etc.)
7. Community services:
   Schools
   Churches
   Recreation
   Hospitals and medical services
   Hotels, motels, and convention centers
   Roads, highways, and transportation systems
   Housing availability and rental rates
   Income and indebtedness of community
   Attitude of community officials
   Community acceptance
   City ordinances and zoning regulations
   Cost of living

Each firm will, of course, weight these factors differently; the weighting itself is an exercise in situational analysis. The existence in a local community of a machine shop that can do precision work is unimportant to a storage and warehousing firm, but very important to a development firm that fabricates mock-ups and models.

In undertaking a study of site location, the management of a firm is actually asking how its organization will fit into the local environment. Are the operational needs of the firm compatible with local conditions? Does the community have adequate supplies of necessary labor, material, and energy inputs? Will the firm be accepted in the community? What are the tax rates? Will the firm overextend current community services? These and many similar questions must be answered before management can make effective decisions on site location. The questions about labor are especially important; site location studies show that labor availability is the most important single consideration. Since labor is generally the most important resource of any organization, that finding is not surprising.

Misjudgment of needs in relation to the environment can have a catastrophic impact on the functioning of an organization. Operating techniques, internal efficiency, and sound management cannot make a firm successful if adequate labor and support services are not available or if transportation costs, taxes, or wage rates are prohibitively high in relation to those of competitors. Site location studies are an attempt to measure many of the important interrelationships between a firm and its environment.

An Aerospace Example

One more example is presented to illustrate the importance of environmental factors in plant operations and to clarify the adaptation concept of situational analysis. It has been emphasized that one of the major responsibilities of management is adaptation of the organization to its environment. That evokes a vision of a manager in the almost helpless position of reacting to powerful environmental forces. But adaptation works both ways. Organizations not only react to environmental forces but frequently create them, as the following example illustrates.

In the 1950s the Department of Defense was actively engaged in contracting with industry for R&D and manufacturing services in an effort to close the missile gap. The effort was complicated by a decision to distribute new missile plants geographically to avoid close proximity to other plants and to urban areas. If they were distributed, the plants would be more difficult targets and population centers would not be endangered. The result was that some plants were built in relatively remote locations where a trained labor force, ample support services, and qualified subcontractors were not available.

One such plant was located in an area where there was no community with over 3,000 residents except for a town of about 10,000 that was 25 miles away. Within a matter of months the plant expanded from a handful of employees to over 6,000. The effect on the local communities was traumatic. Roads and highways became inadequate, telephone facilities were overtaxed, and all other services were suddenly in short supply. Available housing was nonexistent. Schools were immediately overcrowded and land prices escalated. Construction contractors, retailers, and job hunters flooded the area. Communities that had been decreasing in population because of their rural, agrarian setting nearly doubled in a few years. Essentially every plant location factor except climate was adversely affected.

But the effect of the plant on the environment was even more traumatic when, in the early 1960s, missile defense contracting began to taper off. Our national defense arsenal then had enough missiles to destroy 50 percent of Russia's industrial capacity. Within a few years employment at the plant was reduced from over 6,000 to less than 2,000. The impact on the environment was now just the reverse. Housing prices plummeted and FHA foreclosures became common. Schools had excess capacity and a bonded indebtedness now huge in relation to the reduced tax base. Unemployment increased, and retailers felt the pinch of reduced sales. Boom became bust. The scars on the local communities lasted a lot longer than prosperity had lasted.

The Willow Run Example

A classic example of management miscalculation of the environment was the Ford Motor Company decision to build a World War II bomber plant at Willow Run, Michigan. The plant, which required a staff of 42,000, was located in open country 27 miles from its major labor source. To complicate that factor, environmental flexibility was greatly reduced by wartime pressures. Lack of materials for housing, gasoline rationing, shortage of tires, and limited support services all but made operating the plant a fiasco. Turnover was high, and absenteeism frequently averaged 17 percent per day.

Reciprocal Environmental Relationship

The two examples illustrate the strong reciprocal relationship of a firm and its environment. Compatibility of the two is essential if a major disruption of the firm's activities or a major disturbance of environmental elements is to be avoided. Again, the reciprocal relationship is a function of many factors. Larger organizations obviously have a greater impact on the environment than smaller ones. The quantity and quality of environmental resources and institutions affect the degree to which a particular firm or set of firms will affect the environment. One firm pumping sulfur dioxide into the environment may not exceed the capacity of the atmosphere to cleanse itself naturally, but many firms in the same environment will contaminate the atmosphere beyond legal pollution limits. Atmosphere contamination is, of course, an example of a negative impact on the environment.

Dealing with environmental considerations is one of the most trying tasks for a manager. Even though every manager is familiar with the institutions and forces in the environment, management knowledge of how environmental factors affect the internal operations of a firm is more meager than in any other area of administration. Not only is our knowledge limited, but the environment is rapidly increasing in complexity. Technology escalations, population explosions, depletion of resources, and increased governmental regulatory powers have contributed to the complexity. Because of the imponderables in the environment, managerial decision making has in the past been skewed toward emphasis on internal organization. More recently, public attitudes toward ecology, the questioning of profit as a solitary motive, and the impending energy crisis are forcing managers toward a more balanced view in their decision making.

ANALYSIS OF ENVIRONMENTAL CONSTRAINTS

The first difficulty encountered by the businessman in dealing with the environment is that of making sense out of the large number of variables that compose it. Organizations, practices, relationships, trends, and forces combine in institutional confusion. Analysts have tried in many different ways to arrange those variables in a coherent fashion. Some have adopted the economist's view and deal with buyers, sellers, and market forces. Others have focused on the major organizations with which a firm must deal. More recent writers have analyzed the environment from the standpoint of claimants on the firm: stockholders, creditors, employees, customers, suppliers, governments, and communities. Still others have taken the broad approach; they consider the major social forces derived from cultures, technology, economies, governments, and legal systems.

There appear to be at least two layers in the environment. A firm must deal with its customers, suppliers, and competitors in its external relations, but the broader forces, such as technology, affect the firm's customers, suppliers, and competitors as well as the firm itself. Thus there are forces external to the immediate organizational or institutional set of a firm. For the purpose of this analysis, therefore, the environment of a firm is divided into the intermediate or institutional environment and the broader macro environment.

In viewing the intermediate environment of a firm it is convenient to consider the institutional set; a typical example is shown in Figure 7. The major external organizations are those with which the firm must maintain favorable relations if it is to be successful in its accommodation process. Maintaining favorable relationships with those organizations is just as important as maintaining favorable relations among the internal departments or functions. Planning, coordinating, and controlling those relationships deserves as much attention, at least by top-level managers, as managing the internal relationships. The firm must please its stockholders, obtain competent suppliers, satisfy its customers, meet the regulations of governments, and maintain favorable relationships with labor unions if it is to remain competitive or continue to flourish.

Typically the firm handles its external relations by establishing a specialized internal unit to deal with each organization. Procurement or purchasing coordinates suppliers; the labor relations department is the primary contact with labor unions; marketing deals with the customers; marketing and long-range planning groups analyze competitors; and the public relations office maintains relationships with governments and stockholders. Nevertheless, evidence still supports the contention that the typical firm is organized to control internal operations and that external relations are handled on a piecemeal basis. Certainly the external relations are not as integrated, deliberate, or controlled as the internal ones. There is a need for improved methods by which organizations can attain greater knowledge of external pressures and constraints so they can be more responsive to them.

The Intermediate Environment

The organizations that constitute the intermediate environment of the firm are evident, since managers contact them almost every day. The reciprocal relationships and obligations, however, are receiving greater attention and more social significance is being attributed to them. What obligations has a firm to its customers? To its suppliers? What role should it play in the community? What obligations has it to its employees? Should it be concerned with the quality of living of its employees? Should it be concerned with upgrading the experiences of an

Figure 7. **The institutional set of a firm.**

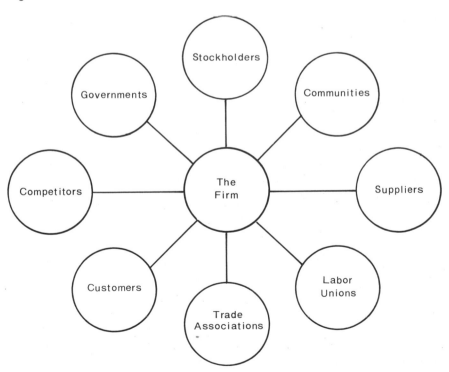

employee in the work situation? All those questions raise the overall issue of the social responsibilities of a business enterprise. They will be considered later in the chapter when the total environment of the firm has been explored.

BROADER ENVIRONMENTAL FORCES

Because the broad macro environment of the firm consists primarily of forces rather than organizations, it is much more difficult to comprehend and assess. Five major forces have been identified; they are economic, technological, political, legal, and social. This list, again, is not intended to be all-inclusive. To those forces, significantly affecting such enterprises as agriculture, construction, and air transportation, weather must be added. The addition emphasizes the necessity for a list of significant factors based upon the unique location, operations, and goals of the firm. However, since economic, technological, political, legal, and social forces are omnipresent, and even occasionally omnipotent, in the environment of firms, they are selected as the primary environmental factors.

Dimensions of the Economic Factor

Since the firm is basically an economic organization, economic forces and institutions tend to predominate in its environment. The world economy and the economy of a country determine the nature of those forces. A firm will function quite differently in a free enterprise economy than in a mixed or socialist one. Within the United States the economic variables of a firm are primarily determined by the nature of its market, and for that reason the U.S. economy is often referred to as a market economy. Economists classify the markets as perfect competition, monopolistic competition, pure oligopoly, differentiated oligopoly, and monopoly depending primarily on the number of buyers and sellers and the similarities of the goods exchanged. Perfect competition and monopoly represent the two extremes on the economic continuum. In perfect competition with an identical product and many producers the seller has no control over price. In a monopoly with only one producer the firm has essentially complete control. Different combinations of control are found in the other markets.

The segmentation of the market based on product differentiation also varies with the market. In pure competition, pure oligopoly, and monopoly there is essentially no differentiation, whereas in monopolistic competition and differentiated oligopoly the products are different. Product differences affect the nature of the supply provided by the firm, and they also have different effects on customer tastes and other factors that determine demand. Supply and demand curves are affected by product differentiation, the number of sellers (competitors), the number of buyers (customers), the price of the products, and many other factors.

Since a firm's basic purpose is to supply goods and services for public consumption, the characteristics of the particular market determine success in accomplishing those objectives. If the number of buyers or sellers gets out of balance or if product differentiation puts the firm at an advantage or disadvantage, the result is disequilibriums that have highly favorable or unfavorable repercussions for the firm. It should be apparent at this point that knowledge of market variables and the characteristics of the markets in which a business enterprise competes are important aspects of success .in managerial decision making.

Because a firm is essentially a profit-making entity, one of its major concerns is the difference between the costs of production of its products or provision of its services and the price it receives for its goods or services in the marketplace. The prices of all the inputs—labor, materials, energy, information, and services—are determined by the economic laws of supply and demand and political laws of governments. The value of a firm's assets, including plant, equipment, and inventory, is determined on much the same basis.

The price a customer is willing to pay for a product is a function of his need or desire for it and his financial resources for purchasing it. Tastes and needs are intangible factors, but personal income, disposable income, and corporate income are tangible ones. The macroeconomist approaches income on a national basis. The total goods and services produced on that basis represent gross national product (GNP), an important indicator of the economic environment in which the firm functions. Increasing GNP, high productivity, and low inflation are favorable signs of consumer ability and desire to purchase and industry ability and desire to produce.

Because the fluctuations or cycles in GNP are a direct indication of the nation's economic health, the government has tended toward strong intervention in economic affairs. Since 1932, taxation and spending and money supply policies have been frequently used to control and reduce GNP fluctuations. The controls have proved effective in avoiding such major depressions as the 1929 crash. However, the more controlled economy has changed the nature of the free enterprise system, and it has made the businessman much more sensitive to the policy vibrations emanating from Washington.

When government had a hands-off policy regarding the economy, business could have a narrow economic view of the scope of its operations. But as government has extended its regulation of business and learned to exert more control over the economy, business interests have had to broaden to include government. Thus the roles of both business and government are expanding. To some degree, of course, the economic, social, and political problems of a society are the concern of all the major institutions in the society. They have no walls between them; instead, they blend together in ways that make it impossible to confine organizations and institutions to any one segment of national life. To draw a line between the interests of business and the interests of government is difficult indeed.

Economic forces have implications for the manager of a business firm that are too numerous to enumerate; they are involved in essentially every decision a manager makes. One of the important activities of a firm is to forecast conditions of the economy and the marketplace so that its managers can make appropriate production, inventory, and facility decisions. If the government is introducing tight money policies, the times are wrong for expanding production of products the sale of which requires extensive consumer credit; if GNP is turning downward and a firm markets a durable good, the times are highly inappropriate for building up a finished goods inventory; if construction costs are inflated and unemployment is increasing in the segment of the population that includes the customers for a firm's product, some rethinking about plant expansion is called for. Production schedules, income statements, balance sheets, and sales forecasts are still the basic tools of the entrepreneur.

Economic forces affect not only tangible resource and financial factors but also such intangibles as the attitude and performance of employees. That is primarily because of the mobility of labor markets under the influence of economic conditions. When opportunities for employment are numerous, a worker is more mobile, less willing to accept work conditions he considers undesirable, and more prone to absenteeism. As the job market becomes tighter, there is a tendency for employees to conform more to the organization, to be less willing to take risks, and to seek greater security.

Technology as an External Factor

In Chapter 6 technology was evaluated as an internal force. It was noted that James D. Bright, professor at the University of Texas, after extensive studies on technology and innovation, concluded that technology is probably the most powerful force in today's business environment. It is a fundamental fact of history that technology has changed the balance of nature. In the past two or three centuries the change has been more drastic than in the preceding thousands of years. Since the industrial revolution man has dominated life on earth in a fashion that is incomparable to early eras. He has put the massive resources of the world to work for his benefit. Within a few hundred years, almost a blink of the eye in the world's existence, he has changed the whole surface of the world and has manifested his superiority over other forms of life; he has done so with technological innovation as the driving force. A world that took billions of years to evolve has been shackled by massive increases in human population, the harnessing and utilization of energy and material resources, and the extension of human power through machines. Man's physical energy alone would not result in dominance. His control of machines and natural energy resources provides a vast multiplier of human power, which has been responsible for the conquest.

Of course, not all of the results of technology are beneficial. Industrialization has resulted in the contamination of waters, the polluting of the air, and the scarring of the earth's surface. It has also threatened other forms of life, which has disrupted the balance of nature. It has forced us to consider the earth as a spaceship on which limited quantities of resources and living space are available. The days of plunder of the planet are over. Man's growth and expansion threaten to be his undoing, especially if nuclear holocausts cannot be avoided.

Like economic systems, technology is a pervasive force in the environment of a firm. Business organizations, especially those based upon high resource utilization and machine processing, are dependent upon the evolving technology. Competing in a marketplace is not only economic but technological. Product, processing, and marketing improvements receive their impetus from technological advance.

As indicated earlier, technological assessment and forecasting are still a largely undeveloped art. Many figures, consisting primarily of estimates by experts in the field, are used in an attempt to evaluate the technological revolution. Derek Price, the historian of science, estimates that 80 to 90 percent of all the scientists who have ever lived are alive today. The knowledge of the world is said to be doubling every 10 years. Product lines that used to last for 10 to 15 years in the marketplace now often have a life of 5 years or less. Also, 90 percent of all productivity increases in organizations have been attributed to technology.

The time lag from scientific discovery to manufacture of product was 112 years for photography. For the telephone it was roughly half that, but in recent years the integrated circuit was developed in only three years. The pace of technology has affected the pace of development of our entire civilization. The business firm has been largely responsible for that pace, since science typically finds expression in the technological applications of industrial enterprises.

The significant effect that the pace of technological advance has on management was keenly appraised by Enthoven and Smith after their experiences in the Department of Defense.

> But something new has been happening since World War II. Science and technology have "taken off" and are now in a period of rapid, accelerated growth . . . . Before World War II, we did not plan on technological change; we merely adjusted to it. Now we are forced to plan on it. We are debating the extent to which inventions can be scheduled, and we have weapon systems that are obsolete while still in development.[1]

That statement concerns the recent big change, but historians have long since noted the influence of technology. The railroads provided the thrust that revolutionized the United States in the last half of the nineteenth century. They provided the mobility that has characterized the nation ever since; they opened up vast areas of the country, especially to industrial expansion. Air and automotive transport had almost the same impact in the first half of the twentieth century.

Before World War II the manager could keep competitive and current by merely reacting to technology. Now, however, the pace of change and the rewards of anticipating change have become so great that management can no longer merely react to technology and be successful. Firms with products or processes that are technological in nature are now pressured to forecast change so they can synchronize their organizations with the advances that take place.

In recent years technological assessment has been the subject of many conferences, papers, and committee reports. Coping with science and technology has become the concern of government, business, science, and social groups. All that culminated in the establishment by Congress of the Office of Technology Assessment. The Office is charged with forecasting the trends of technology, including the harmful side effects.

Implied by technological assessment is an attempt to control and direct emerging technologies to maximize the public benefits while minimizing the public risks. To date most of the assessments have been made on an after-the-fact or hit-or-miss basis rather than based on established criteria or any deliberate methodology. One of the attempts to assess on a before-the-fact basis involved the supersonic transport. However, lack of methods and criteria, as well as political bickering, hamstrung the analysts. There is little doubt that technology is a prime mover in social history and a prime causal factor in the change process displayed by industrial organizations. The objective of technological assessment is to make technology more our servant than our master.

Political and Legal Forces

Even though political and legal forces are shown separately in the situational model diagram, Figure 3, they will be combined for analytical purposes. Governments are the primary representation of political forces in our society; and since governments pass the laws that affect business, it is difficult to separate government from laws for discussion purposes.

Like the other variables in the macro environment of the firm, political influences have ramifications affecting essentially every undertaking of an industrial enterprise. For that reason the role of political forces in the environment of a firm is difficult to summarize. Also, there are several different common methods of analyzing political constraints. One favored by political scientists is to analyze the major organizations and vested interests that affect how a society is controlled and governed. That is the pluralistic approach of attempting to understand all of the organizations that exist in society and how they gain power or exert influence by pressing their particular interests on governments and political organs. The focus is on policy making and all of the political entanglements and power struggles that take place as a part of that process.

The primary lesson of that approach for business organizations is that the policies of government and the direction in which government is moving—including the modification of our capitalist system—are determined by the groups and publics that bring their influence to bear directly or indirectly on government administrators and politicians. If business withdraws from the competition in the political arena, it forfeits its major opportunity to affect its own environment. The firm is basically an economic institution and not a political entity, but governments are influenced by the major interests and needs of society. Business is clearly one of those major interests, and more than a superficial awareness of that fact is required of managers if business is to have its political muscle felt.

Instead of the power-policy approach, political forces can be viewed in the more traditional way by examining the institutions of government and their role in society. That involves an analysis of the various laws and regulations that make up governments and the functions of the various government agencies. The approach is easier to apply in an attempt to enumerate the wide variety of purposes and functions of governments. For that reason it will be adopted in this analysis.

Based on that approach, government in its relationship to business has four interrelated but distinctive roles. In reviewing those roles, the United States is taken as the example and peacetime rather than war is assumed. Government, at one and the same time, is a

Promoter of business interests.

Regulator of business and its interests.

Buyer of business services and products.

Manager of operations that result in goods and services, some of which are used by business and some of which compete with business.

Governments are the suprasystems of society: they can impose their authority structure in all-embracive fashion on other institutions. Since governments are changing, adaptive systems, there is no "normal" example that can be used to identify the role of government. Such identification is possible only by reviewing the role of governments during the past five or ten years, which constitute a stage in the evolution of political institutions.

Government as a Promoter

Various segments of our economy have received major assistance from governments. Notable among them is agriculture. The price of commodities is established and supported by the government; surplus commodities are purchased by the government; and direct subsidies are paid by the government through such programs as the soil bank. Also, shipping firms and airlines have for several decades been paid subsidies for carrying U.S. mail, and the cost of the initial atomic energy power reactors was shared by the government. Indirect subsidies to promote business take such forms as depletion allowances and accelerated depreciation in taxation. Other indirect assistance to promote business is provided by highway and airport construction, harbors, irrigation and flood control, and protective tariffs. The Small Business Administration (SBA) has been established as an agency to foster and aid business by such means as loans, technical assistance, and information services.

All the preceding examples illustrate one or another of government's roles in promoting business, but probably the most important role of all is in R&D funding. In 1943 national expenditures for R&D were approximately $5 billion. By 1970 they had grown to approximately $27 billion, or by a factor of over 5. In 1953 approximately 60 percent of R&D was funded by industry and 40 percent by government. With the increase in government missile and defense research, those percentages were reversed a decade later. However, government funding dropped to 44 percent of the total by 1970, when federal research remained fairly level and industrial research was continuing to grow.

The hand of the government in research and technology is very substantial, since research projects supported by the government determine to a significant extent the manner in which our national research capability is utilized. Government-supported R&D is also an aid to commercial projects carried on by industry. Airframe companies, electronics firms, and many other hardware manufacturers have improved their commercial products by applying knowledge and capability gained through R&D projects they conducted for the government.

Government as a Regulator

Government establishes the rules by which industrial firms must abide as they carry on their activities. Those regulations require conformance on the part of businesses, but they also protect business from unfair practices on the part of competitors or suppliers. Some of the most extensive laws of the federal government are aimed at restricting the monopoly power of business combinations. That legislation started with the Sherman Antitrust Act in 1890, and it has been supplemented several times by other legislation. However, the legislation has been only partially effective. It has not had nearly the impact upon industry that the fiscal and monetary policies of the government used to regulate the economy have had. By increasing or decreasing public expenditures and by increasing or decreasing the amount of taxation, the federal government has pushed funds into the economy through pump priming or siphoned them from the economy to control inflation. The actions of the Federal Reserve Board in affecting the money supply have also served to heat up or cool off the economy, which has had all of the ramifications discussed earlier.

Besides the Antitrust Division of the Department of Justice, many federal agencies have been established to regulate industry. Chief among them is the Federal Trade Commission, which has broad responsibilities relating to deceptive advertising, unfair competition, and price fixing. Public utilities, firms "affected with a public interest," and natural monopolies have been regulated to a much greater extent than other firms.

Most of the transportation industry is regulated by the Interstate Commerce Commission, which has power to establish rates, approve entrance, extension, or abandonment of new lines or services, require safe and adequate service, and approve mergers or changes in capitalization. Air transportation comes under control of the Federal Aviation Agency and the Civil Aeronautics Board. The Federal Power Commission combines with state agencies to control electrical utilities. The Federal Communications Commission has control over radio and television communication, and the securities market is regulated by the Securities and Exchange Commission.

Many of the government agencies were established in the 1930s, when some of the industries were reaching maturity or when operational abuses had become intolerable and government intervention was therefore popular. Labor relations came under regulation through the National Labor Relations Act of 1935, which was modified by the Taft-Hartley Act of 1947. In the 1960s public concern shifted to ecology considerations and the Environmental Protection Agency was established to set pollution standards and institute other controls. More recently, in the 1970s, wage and price controls were adopted to dampen inflation.

A vast web of regulations covers essentially every aspect of business activities. All of the resource inputs of a firm are regulated, and the most comprehensive regulations concern the hiring of the workforce. Many internal operations are also regulated; examples are financial reporting, safety standards, and procurement practices. The marketplace is tightly regulated in regard to pricing policies, competitive practices, labeling laws, and marketing techniques. The regulations are so great in number and so complex in their relations that businessmen find it difficult to know what they are, let alone keep abreast of the latest additions.

Government as a Buyer

The federal government is by far the economy's largest single customer; collectively, governments at the various levels purchase nearly 25 percent of the gross national product. The federal government itself directly contracts with industry for goods and services that amount to 25 percent of its expenditures. The largest single purchasing agency is the Department of Defense. The National Aeronautics and Space Administration and the Atomic Energy Commission are other major purchasers of goods and services.

Many industries are highly reliant on government purchases; and when federal appropriations for that purpose are restricted or expanded, the entire industry is affected in the same manner. State and local government procurements have so increased in recent years that they now rival federal purchases.

The government market is a controversial one because of the associated controls and regulations as well as the instability, especially in the defense sector. However, as long as governments account for one-fourth of all expenditures for goods and services, they will be a dominant influence in the marketplace.

Government as a Manager

The government manages massive resources and major industrial operations in competition with industry; it also provides some goods and services directly to industry. Approximately one-third of the United States is public domain and is managed by such agencies as the Bureau of Land Management, the Forest Service, and the National Park Service.

In 1955 the Hoover Commission identified over 19,000 commercial and industrial installations in civilian agencies and about 5,000 in the Department of Defense. Under the "arsenal concept" many defense items are still designed, produced, and maintained by governmental units. The nature of the goods and services provided industry is indicated by the following examples: The Tennessee Valley Authority and local governments provide electric power; numerous agencies such as the Federal Housing Administration either provide or insure loans; there are a variety

116

of federal banks; and the government is involved in many different insurance and credit programs.

Of the four roles mentioned, that of the federal government as a manager is currently the least important one to business. However, continued problems with industries such as the railroads could increase the pressures for nationalization and quickly alter the government's managerial role.

Increasing Government Intervention in Business

Since 1930 there has been a drastic change in the role of government in business. The laissez faire policy is now in disfavor, and the public is much more receptive to government intervention than it once was. Many reasons have been given for the change, but basically the public does not want a return to the uncertainties or potential abuses of the 1930s. Also, as the economy has provided a higher standard of living, social goals have tended to become more important in relation to economic ones. Social legislation thus has a broadened base. In addition, the complexity of an advancing society tends to generate the need for regulations. For example, atomic energy developed sufficiently as a science to make production of power in an atomic reactor economically feasible. The result was a need for regulation because of the health hazards involved.

Whereas business and government were once considered to be competing institutions, they are now perceived to resemble partners. Man's walk on the moon could have been made possible only by a partnership of business and government. The Committee for Economic Development (CED), a forward-looking group of 200 businessmen with some educators, predicts growing cooperation between the two. In 1971 the CED said:

> The converging of two trends—the business thrust into social fields, and government's increasing use of market incentives to induce even greater business involvement—is gradually bringing these two powerful institutions into a constructive partnership for accelerating social progress. The emerging partnership is more than a contractual relationship between a buyer and seller of services. Fundamentally, it offers a new means for developing the innate capabilities of a political democracy and a private enterprise economy into a new politico-economic system capable of managing social and technological change in the interest of a better social order.[2]

The CED views the government's role as the establishment of national goals and priorities. The role of business is to use its management skills in developing and administering social and economic programs. Whatever the outcome, there can be little doubt that the role of government is not likely to diminish and that a mixed economy featuring more cooperation between government and business, such as we see in atomic energy, communication satellites, and space research, is the trend of the future.

117

Sociocultural Considerations

Every organization takes on the characteristics of the larger society of which it is a part. Organizations conceived in a particular culture inherit the characteristics of that culture, and are affected by the values, mores, and behavior patterns of that society. In fact, as Katz and Kahn state, "organizations obtain their legitimation through their acceptance of the values of the larger society." [3]

One of the major variables in an organization is the culture from which it evolved. Parallel organizations in different countries will function differently because of the difference in cultures. Multinational corporations have often experienced temporary failure when they attempted to transport American managerial systems overseas. Participative leadership styles are normally not effective in highly authoritarian cultures. In Japan, where employment with a company is normally lifelong, personnel policies are considerably different than in the United States. In South America attitudes toward work affect a manager's actions. There are many other examples of how cross-cultural differences determine the principles a manager applies in a particular situation.

The values, attitudes, educational levels, behavior patterns, and demographic characteristics of a society constitute important attributes of the social setting of an organization. They serve as the standards or affect the establishment of the standards by which actions are measured in a society. Those standards gradually evolve over time and reflect the revised expectations of the people in a society. Those changes are a current challenge to the basic premises of the American business firm. The question of the social responsibilities of the firm has developed as a major issue in the 1960s. What responsibility does a firm have for unemployment? To help overcome urban blight? To improve race relations? To employ minorities? To help its employees develop into better human beings? To aid education? To improve the quality of living?

Not many years ago the response to all those questions would have been that the firm is an economic institution; since the problems are social and not economic, the responsibility of the firm is very minimal. In recent years, however, attitudes have been changing. In a 1970 Opinion Research Corporation poll 60 percent of those questioned consider it a main responsibility of business to keep the environment clean and free of pollution. Business functions by consent of the public; and as the needs of society have become increasingly social, the public has looked more and more to business to help satisfy those needs.

Part of the transformation has been brought about by the changing conditions in society. In the 1930s, when the United States experienced 25 percent unemployment and 60 percent of the population was on a substandard of living, economic needs were primary. That is consistent with Maslow's need hierarchy applied on a societal rather than an individual basis. Maslow, a leading American psychologist, has said that physical needs are primary until they are satisfied at a minimal level and then social and achievement needs take over in importance. Economic needs are primary for a society also, but other needs become relatively more important when economic needs reach minimum acceptable sustenance levels. Today, when unemployment hovers at the 5 percent level and poverty is confined to 10 percent of our population, social needs become relatively more important and economic needs less important, although the two are definitely interrelated. The tremendous capacity of the United States to supply an adequate standard of living has focused more of our national concern on the social problems that remain unresolved.

It is becoming increasingly more difficult for business firms to consider their roles as solely economic. Approximately 80 percent of the people who work in the United States work directly for business organizations. A significant portion of their waking hours and their outlets for self-expression are tied up with their employers. Also, business is certainly one of the most powerful institutions in our society, especially when its reservoir of managerial skill is considered. For those reasons it is hard for business to ignore the problems of society, particularly since there is a reciprocal relationship between the two.

Because business cannot function unless the environment is conducive to business activity, it has a vested interest in maintaining an environment that is hospitable to business. Society, on the other hand, has a vested interest in the productive and managerial capacities of business; it needs the tremendous capacity and know-how of business to solve its problems. Viewed from either direction, business cannot turn its back on the problems of society. Institutions that corner 80 percent of the manpower capacity and skills of a society have a responsibility to use that capacity to solve societal ills. That is not to imply that business should assume the functions of government. Government should determine the policies and objectives, but business should be paid on a profit basis to use its capacity to help direct and manage programs to improve all aspects of society, social as well as economic.

One of the biggest problems in that regard is the lack of social indicators. We have widely accepted, precise, objective standards for measuring the economic contribution of a firm. For that reason our judgment of a firm tends to focus on the information that is available and of traditional use—that is, on the financial issues. Social indicators are almost totally lacking. How do you measure the social contribution of a firm? How do you measure the value of the most important resource of a firm, its human assets? How can social and economic measures be equated? Until better social indicators are developed, the contributions of the firm in its expanded area of activity will be subject to uncertainties that will make decision making difficult and evaluation highly subjective.

SITUATIONAL APPROACHES TO ENVIRONMENTAL FACTORS

One of the biggest challenges to a manager engaged in situational analysis is to interpret environmental constraints. With the aid of planning and control systems, financial systems, and management information systems, a manager has at his fingertips considerable data on the internal variables of the firm. However, he normally lacks such information on external variables. Also, as emphasized earlier, the structure of the organization is set up to manage internally. A manager's training and advancement in a firm are centered around internal constraints and problems. Small wonder that managers are so little prepared for external considerations as they advance to the top of an organization.

In political science studies it has been found that major changes in the form and functions of government are normally associated with some crisis such as a war or major depression. In a study of the history of business firms also it can be noted that major external changes are reflected in major internal changes. General Motors serves as an interesting example. William C. Durant, its founder, was originally a manufacturer of two-wheel horse-drawn carts. Technological advance created a major change in the environment: the internal-combustion engine was introduced into the marketplace. Durant successfully adapted his two-wheel cart organization to the horseless carriage. He was a highly successful marketing manager, and his firm rapidly grew in the early 1900s.

The next major change in the environment occurred in 1910, when a slight business recession found G.M. short of cash. Durant was forced out of management. Within five years he was back as president only to face another external crisis, World War I. Again the corporation successfully adapted. Automotive production dropped off because of the shortage of materials and the demands of military orders. Excess capacity would have developed, because the internal-combustion engine was not yet a vital war instrument. To compensate for the reduction in automotives, General Motors turned to the manufacture of tractors and refrigerators. A short time later an environmental change once again caught Durant short. The recession of 1920 found General Motors overinventoried in automobiles and Durant was displaced for a second time.

A study of the history of large corporations reveals that environmental considerations account for many of the major changes that occur within a firm. Internal management problems that can be tolerated under steady conditions in the environment reach the breaking point when some great change occurs in environmental factors.

INTERRELATIONSHIP OF ENVIRONMENTAL FACTORS

One final point regarding environmental constraints must be made. The environment cannot be accurately evaluated by segregating its institutions or forces and examining each one separately. The major influences on the status of any external variable are the other external variables; there is as constant an interplay among the external variables of the firm as among the internal ones.

Examples of interaction are not hard to find. The status of the economy affects personal income and unemployment, which directly help create or resolve social problems. The most important factor affecting international relations in the past half century or perhaps in the history of the world has been a technological innovation, atomic explosives. The most important factor in the past half century affecting economic considerations has been governmental adoption of fiscal and monetary policies. One of the major influences on social values and education has been another technological innovation, television. As has been shown earlier, one of the big factors in technological advance has been government expenditures for research and development. Finally, one of the two or three most significant barometers of any society, population change, has been strongly affected by technological advances in medical science, food processing, and birth control. All these interactions force a firm to be in a constant state of redefinition, which presents the adaptation challenge to the manager.

nine
leadership styles and behavior

THE ENVIRONMENTAL FACTORS enumerated in Chapter 8 provide the final element of the situational model of management. They are part of the construct in which the external and internal environments of the firm are interrelated. Many questions arise at this point. Of what benefit is the construct to the practitioner? How does it help him make decisions? How does it alter his utilization of management principles and concepts? Will it affect how he leads in his organization? Will it affect the selection of managers? The purpose of this chapter is to attempt to answer those questions.

APPROACHES TO LEADERSHIP

Of all the subfields of management, situational theory has been associated with leadership styles and concepts for the longest time. Prior to World War II Mary Parker Follett, Kurt Lewin, Ronald Lippitt, and Chester Barnard, among others, noted that leadership is situational and that no one best style of leadership exists. Following World War II, in 1948, Ralph Stogdill conducted an extensive study of the personal factors that make leadership situational. By 1950 the contingency concept of leadership was gaining wide support. Many of the best known national experts on leadership since that time, such as Douglas McGregor, Fred Fiedler, and Rensis Likert, have been of the situationalist school. The concept is therefore widely recognized by management writers, but, surprisingly, the theoretical framework of the approach has never been fully developed or elaborated.

The situational theory of leadership evolved primarily as a reaction to the failure of the traitist approach. Early management writers and researchers attempted to uncover a set of traits that typified successful leaders. The assumption was that, once the traits that constituted the one best leadership style were established, management selection could be reduced to finding people with the proper physical, intellectual, and personality traits. Also, leadership training would then consist of an attempt to develop those traits in potential leaders.

Over the past 70 years, hundreds of studies have been conducted but no universal set of traits has been established. In one summary of over a hundred studies only 5 percent of the traits were found in four or more studies. Certain traits that seemed to be primary ingredients of success in some situations were of limited importance in others. Therefore, the conclusion was reached that it is the demands of the situation that dominate, and leaders are successful only when their particular traits happen to fit those demands.

The consequence, then, has been wide acceptance of situationalist theory. Even so, most management writers have not attempted to say

124

specifically what that theory consists of other than to say that it involves three sets of variables: the characteristics of the leader, the characteristics of the followers, and the characteristics of the situation. Normally the situation is considered to be most important because it contains the greatest number of variables, but until recently little attempt has been made to classify in a common framework the range of variables that constitute the situation.

In 1960 Douglas McGregor, in his widely read book *The Human Side of Enterprise,* identified four major variables involved in leadership: (1) the characteristics of the leader, (2) the attitudes, needs, and other personal characteristics of the followers, (3) characteristics of the organization, such as its purpose, its structure, and the nature of the tasks to be performed, and (4) the social, economic, and political milieu. McGregor's approach established the basic framework of the situation. However, the utility of the framework was limited because the specific dimensions of the variables were not elaborated sufficiently for a determination of how those variables dictate specific courses of managerial action.

The contributions of one more individual must be noted; they are the research studies of Fred Fiedler as summarized in his book *A Theory of Leadership Effectiveness.* From those studies Fiedler became convinced that leadership performance depends as much on the organization as on the leader: "Except perhaps for the unusual case, it is simply not meaningful to speak of an effective leader or of an ineffective leader; we can only speak of a leader who tends to be effective in one situation and ineffective in another." [1]

In his studies Fiedler focuses on three group or task dimensions that make it easy or difficult for the leader to exert influence on group performance: the leader-member relations, the task structure, and the leader's position power. His studies have gone a long way toward popularizing the contingency theory of leadership. However, in the conclusion of his book he notes that, "above all, we require a better method for measuring the favorableness of the leadership situation." [2] He calls for scales that will take the factors that are likely to affect that favorableness into account.

The Nature of Leadership

One of the basic differences between the traditional approaches to leadership taken by behavioral writers and the management approach utilized in this book relates to the nature of leadership. Psychologists and sociologists have restricted leadership to the interpersonal process by which an individual gets others to follow his direction. The essence of leadership, they say, consists in stimulating and influencing others to become followers. The study of leadership is therefore very closely related to the study of power and emphasizes the emotional rather than the rational element.

The managerial approach to leadership based on situational analysis is much broader. Granted the tenets of systems theory, the leader's role is that of adapting the organization to external forces. Situationalists criticize traditional approaches to leadership for the same reasons they criticize traditional principles of formal organization. In both the internal relationships of a firm or group are considered and the external relationships are virtually ignored. Leadership is more than just the stimulation of followers to contribute to the attainment of organizational goals; it involves relating the organization to external factors. Growth, advancement, and goal achievement are not strictly internal problems; they have important external dimensions.

A consequence of the broader view was the need for a proper interpretation of the opportunities in the marketplace or environment, given the constraints represented by other organizations and external forces. The leader is the visionary who accurately interprets those dynamic external factors and steers the organization toward the potentialities he envisions. He encourages the establishment of organizational goals that are consistent with the needs of the organization and the individual members. When he is successful in that regard, feelings of cooperation and commitment are generated within the group.

In leadership analysis one of the fundamental distinctions that becomes critical is that between a leader and an efficient administrator. The difference is detailed in Table 3. The efficient administrator is one who effectively handles the internal operations of the organization. He keeps the enterprise functioning by coordinating, expediting, and monitoring the organization's existing activities. The leader is more the visionary. He keeps attuned to the direction in which the organization is moving, and he attempts to change that direction in response to developments in the broader environment. He concentrates on the process by which the goals of the organization are redefined, and he stimulates the membership of the organization to seek high levels of goal attainment.

By that it should not be assumed that the leader has a free hand in redefining goals, modifying the basic mission, or even making fundamental policy decisions. Nothing could be further from the truth. He must conform to external forces, group pressures, and the opinions of power figures in much of what he does. He is the one who properly interprets those forces or conditions and pursues a course of action that will be successful within their constraints.

The leader often has personal convictions or biases that are contrary to the direction in which he is attempting to move the organization. However, he recognizes that pursuing his own convictions may result in the alienation of his membership or a potential setback in dealing with outside groups. The head of an organization may not want to see women in management positions; but if cultural norms favor that change, he will likely open the way for it. The president of a university might personally feel that agricultural research should be deemphasized in his institution; but if the university gains its support from primarily rural areas and if important alumni and members of the board of regents represent agricultural interests, he is unlikely to take a strong stand in that regard. Heads of governments are known for taking specific positions on political issues during a campaign but pursuing a far different course of action when they assume office and the various political realities come to bear upon them.

A leader is always aware that to maintain his leadership position he must maintain the support of his followers. He attempts to shape and mold group opinion, but he frequently discovers that external or internal pressures force him to modify his personal preferences for what he considers to be the good of the organization. The effective leader avoids the impasse of win-or-lose situations; again, his challenge is situational.

Table 3. Characteristics of a leader and an efficient administrator.

Leader	*Efficient Administrator*
Continually defines and redefines institutional role and purpose.	Efficiently processes materials, information, reports, etc.
Concerned with the adaptation of the organization to forces in the environment. Promotes desired change.	Keeps organization functioning effectively at its current level.
Emphasizes goal setting and long-range planning. Steers the organization toward his vision of the future.	Handles daily activities or chores in an expeditious manner.
Defends institutional integrity and protects the organization from external threats.	Coordinates and integrates ongoing activities.
Focuses on promoting the welfare of the entire organization by minimizing or balancing internal vested interests.	Maintains the current status of the organization.
Plays a major role in influencing organizational behavior and establishing organizational climate.	Works toward activity, not results.
Stimulates followers to contribute to the attainment of organizational goals.	Is known for "getting things done" but not for generating change.

He must properly interpret the desires of subgroups and informal leaders and the pressures of external groups and forces. He needs to pursue a course of action that blends those forces and is broadly interpreted as success for the organization. That is the way he maintains his power position. He is engaged in a balancing act—the art of successful compromise. Yet it is by compromise that the successful leader can wield unusual personal influence in gaining support of the major elements within the organization.

Sources of Leadership Power

The power of the leader is derived from many sources. Like any other phenomenon in organization behavior, it is a function of situational circumstance. In the formal business organization power has typically been attributed to the authority associated with position. The power of a supervisor, for example, was felt to be a function of the authority he had to direct his subordinates and the sanctions he had to force compliance. Now, the capacity to satisfy someone else's needs through the rewards or penalties that a supervisor has at his disposal is certainly an important source of power. If he can increase or decrease pay, assign desired or undesired tasks, or promote or terminate a subordinate, the supervisor controls important sources of need satisfaction that influence the behavior of the individuals subject to his authority.

However, in addition to position-based influence, knowledge-based influence is also a potent source of control. People tend to listen to and be influenced by the expert. If they consider a supervisor to be knowledgeable, they accept his direction—not necessarily because he has formal authority, but because they feel it will result in the most desirable outcome. No one likes to engage in effort he feels is misdirected or wasted. Thus young college graduates who are thrust into the position of supervisor must normally win the respect of old-timers before they can exert a large amount of influence over them. In today's business environment, in which capricious acts of supervision are restricted by union-management agreements and other regulations, authority is not sufficient of itself to create a strong supervisor. The supervisor must be also accepted as being fair and knowledgeable by the work group.

Power can also arise from personality traits or physical attributes. An individual may have power because his group considers him to be dynamic, decisive, or likable. Alternatively, his power may derive from social background, control of resources, or monetary worth. The ability to influence others is a function of how important those particular variables are in the situation. Position-based influence may be negligible in a group of teenagers, who have little respect for authority, but it may be substantial in a group of older employees, who are part of an earlier culture that emphasized authority. The expert knowledge of a chemist may not bear much weight in the Wednesday night bowling league, but it will be of considerable influence in meetings of the local chemical society. The relevance of the authority and the knowledge of any particular leader will vary with the group, as will the sources of his status. The reaction of people to these factors will also differ, which makes the power of the leader entirely a function of situational factors and prohibits broad generalizations about sources of power in organizations.

THE EFFECTIVENESS OF APPROACHES TO LEADERSHIP

One of the primary conclusions drawn from situational theory is that different situations dictate the need for different types of leaders. Thus one of the objectives of situational analysis is to interpret situations accurately so that proper leaders can be appointed or so that the leaders might engage in specific behavior that will be effective in the situations. To make those determinations of value, however, there must be some way to classify types of leaders or acts of leadership. Several ways have been used in the past. The most common way is based on the manner in which the leader exercises the authority of his position. Another way is to classify on the basis of concern as a leader. Leaders with a high concern for production are said to be task-oriented or job-centered leaders; those who emphasize effective working relationships with groups are said to be relationship-oriented or people-oriented supervisors. However, since most of the research and literature have been based on the leader's exercise of authority, that approach will be followed in this analysis.

Table 4 presents a summary of the three common leadership styles, which have been extensively considered in management literature since before World War II. Originally the three styles were referred to as authoritarian, democratic, and laissez faire, but those terms have political and economic value connotations that tend to make them misleading. Accordingly the more neutral terms of directive, participative, and free-rein are preferable.

The Directive Leader

The directive leader relies on his authority to accomplish the work of the organization, and he tends to centralize that authority in his own hands. He keeps close control over his direct subordinates; to do so he makes all of the management and many of the operating decisions. He

129

usually dictates activity steps one at a time, which permits subordinates little freedom of action. The subordinates are thus highly dependent upon the leader, and they feel their performance is judged by their obedience to the leader's directives. The leader's entire orientation is toward the tasks performed or the productivity of the group. The feelings or interests of subordinates are usually secondary to the efficiency expectations that are fundamental to the organization.

Under a directive leader the subordinate is typically motivated by the financial income, which satisfies his subsistence needs, and by the leader's ability, based on personal qualities, to inspire him. The leader's primary

Table 4. Comparison of leadership styles.

Directive	*Participative*	*Free-rein*
Leader makes most of the decisions.	Subordinates are involved in decisions.	Subordinates make decisions.
Little freedom of action is permitted.	Leader fosters some independence.	Subordinates have almost complete independence.
Leader uses power and discipline.	Leader tries to persuade, not force.	Reliance is on self-control.
Activity is leader-centered.	Activity is group-centered.	Focus is on individual activity.
Leader utilizes one-way communication.	Leader encourages two-way communication.	Communication is free and open.
Leader stays aloof from group.	Leader is involved in group.	Leader is not identifiable in the group.
Leader has little concern for subordinate's feelings.	Leader considers subordinate's feelings.	Subordinate's feelings predominate.
Leader takes full responsibility.	Leader shares power and responsibility.	The individual is responsible.
Leader's role is to provide direction.	Leader's role is group involvement.	Leader's role is to provide support resources.
Leader seeks stable, predictable situation.	Leader is more flexible and adaptive.	Internal environment is highly flexible.
Employee orientation is obedience.	Employee orientation is cooperation.	Orientation is individual performance.
Psychological result is dependency.	Psychological result is participation.	Psychological result is independence.

reliance on authority frequently results in the use of force or threat to keep subordinates active or busy. The emphasis is on order and conformity, which tends to develop a short-term perspective in subordinates. But if the leader relies solely on his power and the use of threat to accomplish work, subordinates can be alienated. Sometimes they deliberately retaliate by undercutting the supervisor or engaging in slowdowns. Directive leadership is certainly an effective method of supervision in many situations, but it must be delicately handled or the subordinates will be inclined to desert the organization or ignore its objectives.

The Participative Leader

The participative style of leadership represents the middle ground. The leader makes and is responsible for the major decisions of the organization, but he seeks to involve subordinates to the degree they can contribute. However, he does not seek involvement purely for its own sake. He is convinced that when conditions permit, the subordinate is more productive and can increase his contribution to the organization if he is given some independence and if he participates in major activities. The premise is that if individuals are permitted to function more on their own, they will take more responsibility for their work and derive greater feelings of recognition and self-satisfaction from what they do. The appeal is to the psychological need of applying personal skills to activities that are significant to the work of the organization.

The participative leader tends to feel responsible for the results of the organization, and so he makes most of the managerial decisions. He does, however, encourage suggestions from subordinates, and he considers their feelings. He tends to leave the operating or how decisions up to them. As long as his subordinates achieve the results desired, he permits them to make decisions and have freedom of action in the way work is accomplished. The participative leader is more open and adaptive than the directive leader. He injects himself more into group activities, but he never loses his leadership position.

Because the way is more open for them to contribute and for their ideas to be utilized, subordinates of participative leaders are more cooperative in dealing with others and display greater commitment to the goals of the organization. If goals are imposed from outside, there may be little reason to accept them. If, on the other hand, an individual participates in establishing the goals, he is more inclined to identify with the objectives and with the goal-oriented activity of the organization. The normal result is higher morale and better group cohesion. Also, when an individual participates in management processes by recommending courses of action, he develops his managerial skills much faster than someone who is closely directed in all that he does. Generally, better decisions are made because of the ideas and input of subordinates.

Several problems arise from participative leadership. Much more time is needed to involve others in developing a course of action or making a decision. Frequently problems will not wait for such deliberation. Also, if the leader is an innovator and has understanding far superior to that of the group, he will moderate and water down what needs to be done if he seeks consensus. In addition, it is difficult to find executives with a participative leadership temperament. Hard-driving executives are stimulated by feelings of recognition and achievement. To share their power and the spotlight with subordinates is often contrary to their ego needs.

Furthermore, participation is of little value if the subordinates are not informed. Unless subordinates can contribute, group discussions may be little more than the pooling of ignorance. Participation is certainly no panacea; but if the proper conditions exist, it can be a highly effective method of leading a group. Other things being equal, participative leadership is considered by behaviorists to be founded on a sounder theory of human behavior even after the conformity constraints imposed by formalized organizational effort are acknowledged.

The Free-rein Leader

The free-rein style of leadership is infrequently found in business organizations and is therefore of much less significance to this study than the other styles. Most of the attributes of free-rein leadership are just the opposite of those of directive leadership. Subordinates are almost entirely free to pursue their work in the way they wish. They run their own projects and determine their own priorities. They make the decisions, provide whatever coordination with others is necessary, and are essentially 100 percent responsible for what they do. The supervisor's role is to provide the support resources and services necessary for individual activities. Other than resource constraints, there are very few limitations on what the individual does. Free-rein situations normally exist among professional people, so that professional norms and ethics guide what takes place. The professional is considered an expert in his field; and since he is more familiar than anyone else with his activity, the emphasis is on self-control, self-evaluation, and individual responsibility. Free-rein leadership is found scattered in research and development, universities, and specialized activities such as selling.

Free-rein leadership can be highly motivational when the tasks of the organization can be independently handled on an individual basis. It is much more difficult to exercise and far less effective when group coordination is required to accomplish the tasks of the organization. Under a free-rein leader, an organization can drift from a lack of direction, and chaos can result if the leadership style is misapplied. Since most activities in organizations have a high task-sequential interdependence or involve an integration of tasks, the typical leader has little opportunity to utilize free-rein leadership. It is true that free-rein leadership may be found in production activities, but then it usually represents a void in leadership or the absence of leadership and so is not intentional, much less successful.

As indicated earlier, the three leadership styles have commonly been designated as those available to supervision. However, in reality, there are not three, but hundreds of different styles in a continuum with the directive type at one extreme and the free-rein type at the other. There are, in fact, many different varieties of any one style. For instance, the directive style is characterized by the dictatorial autocrat on the extreme left of the continuum and the benevolent autocrat just to the left of the participative leader.

Here the continuum concept is identical with that on which the dimensions of factors in the situational model of management are based. The way in which a supervisor employs his authority is represented by many different points along the continuum. Individuals who exercise authority similarly would be at roughly the same point along the continuum, but no two individuals, of course, exercise authority in identically the same way.

SITUATIONAL ANALYSIS OF LEADERSHIP

In situational analysis the objective is to identify each key factor in the situation by evaluating the dimensions of the factor. Once the situation is mapped, the question becomes that of the course of action or leadership styles that will be effective. In relation to leadership the objective is to identify the dimensions and variables that affect leadership patterns. That is followed by an elaboration of how those different characteristics affect the success of different styles. To that end, each of the factors and applicable dimensions will be analyzed in the sequence in which they were presented in Chapter 3 on the contingency model.

The Purpose Factor and Leadership

The purpose factor affects leadership primarily in relation to the degree to which the people in the organization accept the basic goals and mission of the organization. Actually, it is a combination of the purpose and people factors. If people accept and highly identify with the goals and mis-

133

sion of the organization, a participative or free-rein leadership style is appropriate. However, if they do not identify with the purpose of the organization, other things being equal, they will normally require a more directive type of leader who will apply force to get them to engage in tasks they do not find naturally appealing.

The same thing can be said in relation to the values inherent in the purpose of the organization. If the individual has personal values that are consistent with the basic values of the organization, more participative styles of leadership are appropriate. If, for example, a social worker has personal values that are consistent with the purposes or the values inherent in a welfare organization, he will be much more committed to the work and need not be forced to be productive.

The Task Factor and Leadership

No factor is more important in dictating leadership styles than the task factor. Fiedler, Lawrence and Lorsch, and Hage and Aiken agree that routine, repetitive, production tasks tend to call for a more centralized organization with task-oriented leadership. When tasks are highly routine, specialized, and repetitive in nature, there are few natural motivators. Because the tasks are dull and provide few outlets for creativity, leadership must be more directed toward forcing the work to be accomplished. In fact, routine production situations are today the remaining bastions of directive leadership. Participative styles have been tried in routine production and have had only limited success.

On the other hand, tasks that are varied, complex, and challenging tend to be more motivational, and so participative styles are more appropriate. There will, of course, be variations, because what is challenging for one individual may not be challenging for someone with different skills, needs, and training. However, leadership research tends to support generalizations regarding the routine production situation and the more open, problem-solving R&D one.

Another critical dimension of tasks that affects leadership style is sequential interdependence. People working on an assembly line or in some other situation that requires close coordination of effort typically need more directive leadership. The more tasks must conform to standards or be integrated with the tasks performed by other individuals, the less the permissible freedom of action. On the other hand, tasks that can be performed with a high degree of autonomy can be supervised in participative or free-rein style. Finally, it should be noted that tasks rated high on the dimension of working with people, such as selling, personnel relations, and service activities, normally attract leaders who are people-oriented. Participative styles thus tend to be appropriate.

The Technology Factor and Leadership

If intensive technology characterizes a firm's operations, the tasks are apt to be of the complex, problem-solving kind that must be performed by individuals with technical training. Many of them will call for a professional background. The nature of the tasks and individuals involved makes a participative or free-rein style of leadership appropriate.

Scientific tasks call for leaders who have technical expertise. The professional training of both leaders and followers encourages an open organizational climate in which creativity and innovation are encouraged. Independence of action is fostered and even mandatory if the scientist is engaged in projects in which he is more knowledgeable of the technical details than his supervisor. Scientific laboratories, universities, and R&D operations are normally characterized by permissive, supportive-type leadership. Operations low in technology, such as simple assembly tasks, are characterized by more directive leadership.

The People Factor and Leadership

Several dimensions of the people factor have already been related to task and technology dimensions. Unskilled production workers are more effectively led by directive leaders. Highly skilled scientists perform best under participative or free-rein leaders. The training and skill of the worker represent the two dimensions of people that are most critical in prescribing leadership styles.

The primary prerequisite of participative management is that the people must be knowledgeable enough to contribute. Untrained, summer hires require direction in most of what they do; knowledgeable professionals are insulted by any attempt at detailed direction of their work. Participative styles have been shown to be most effective when the people in the group have relatively equal capability. When the range of capability is wide, the more able people tend to dominate and the de facto result is only limited participation.

The specific traits, emotional makeup, and temperament of people will also affect leadership styles. Studies have shown that people with strong authoritarian tendencies are more likely to accept autocratic, directive leaders. On the other hand, people with strong independence and achievement needs function better under participative leaders. Leaders who have a strong need to be liked and accepted may be inclined to function in the free-rein style.

The expectations of subordinates, peers, and higher-level managers tend to shape and modify all other factors in leadership. If an individual expects the leader to be directive, he is more tolerant of his situation than if he expects the leader to be more permissive. Rensis Likert of the University of Michigan, one of the outstanding researchers in leadership, reaches this conclusion: "The subordinate's reaction to the supervisor's behavior always depends upon the relationship between the supervisory act as perceived by the subordinate and the expectations, values, and interpersonal skills of the subordinate."[3]

The Structure Factor and Leadership

Several of the structure dimensions tend to be associated with specific leadership styles. Formal structure reflects the designers' expectations of how leaders will function; accordingly, the nature of the structure tends to facilitate or hamper a specific style of leadership. For instance, a structure that is highly formalized tends to encourage directive leadership: job descriptions are detailed; activity steps are enumerated; and work methods are prescribed. Thus, the freedom of action of the subordinate is limited and the supervisor has a greater obligation to monitor and control employee performance in accordance with the standards. On the other hand, decentralized structures are more conducive to participative styles. Authority is delegated down the chain of command and subordinates are expected to function with a higher degree of independence.

Span of control also affects leadership. A supervisor with a broad span of control and many subordinates does not have the time to make all the decisions for every employee. Time restrictions force him to grant his subordinates more independence. In contrast, a leader with a small control span can be much more autocratic if he is so inclined. The scale dimension can be associated with leadership styles in the same way. Small size of organization is conducive to directive leadership just as a small span of control is. Geographical dispersion affects control but not quite in the same way. If operations are dispersed, more authority is delegated to the individual on the spot, who is aware of local conditions. That is especially necessary if time is a vital factor in decision making.

The position a person holds in the organization and the role associated with that position are two of the most important structural determinants of leadership style. If an individual holds a line position, he is much more likely to be directive than he would be in a staff capacity. Line officials are expected to provide the direction in the organization, and staff administrators are expected to support them. The expectations that others have regarding the behavior of the incumbent of a particular position constitute the role of that position. If the top managers in the organization, through their interaction with lower-level supervisors, indicate that they expect supervisors to be directive, the latter are inclined to lead in that fashion. The expectations of subordinates influence the supervisor in the same way. If the workers are accustomed to an autocratic leader and they expect the current supervisor to be autocratic, that message is conveyed through their behavior. Generally, that will affect leadership style.

Expectations often result in organizational inbreeding. Over a period of years the top executives may, for example, be highly authoritarian. They develop an organization climate in which supervisors feel that, if they are to be effective leaders, they must be directive leaders. New people coming into the organization soon realize that, to get ahead in supervision, they must please the leaders in the organization, so they copy their leadership styles. In that way the leadership style tends to perpetuate itself. Specific leadership styles are associated with entire industries. That is not wholly the result of inbreeding, of course. It is due also to the nature of the operations performed in the industry and the forces that generate change in the industry.

Essentially every dimension of structure can be associated to some degree with leadership style. One final example has to do with departmentation. Patterns of leadership are affected by whether the firm is organized on a functional, geographical, product, process, or customer basis. Probably product departmentation has the most direct influence on leadership style. In the aerospace industry the matrix form of project management is quite common. In that mixture of functional and product organization, functional departmentation exists in the familiar vertical hierarchy. Thus, engineers report to engineers and production work units report to higher-level production departments.

Cutting horizontally through the aerospace organization are subunits that represent the firm's various programs or products. Engineering is broken down into several smaller groups related to specific products, and so are quality control, production, and the other organizational elements. The subelements associated with a product are coordinated by a program manager who is responsible for the product. The program manager lacks total line authority over the suborganizations, however. His decision-making responsibility is primarily to make work assignments, establish schedules, and allocate resources. Since he does not have total authority, he must rely more upon persuasion than force. Also, his job is to coordinate and integrate a diverse team of specialists whose participation is important because of their specialized knowledge. Thus, participative leadership has the best chance of success.

External Factors and Leadership

The external factors that affect leadership—political, social, economic, and technological forces—are in dynamic interplay. They constantly establish unique conditions that place different demands on leadership. As a result, certain styles are sometimes more effective than others. If external change is slow, the leadership can be sluggish in reaction and the organization will still survive. However, if change is rapid, or especially if crisis conditions occur, far different demands are placed on the leader.

The political parallel furnishes a good analogy. If an international crisis occurs and war breaks out, the president is granted emergency powers by Congress and our democratic society temporarily has dictatorial leadership. The same thing is true of business organizations. If a firm is rapidly losing sales to competitors, its leaders are forced to take more decisive action and a harder line toward compliance. Sometimes a situation will call for new leadership that is not so closely associated with the current way of doing things. In the extreme case the need is even for a leader who will make rapid, resolute, far-reaching decisions in an attempt to turn the organization around.

Time is one of the most important factors in the situational model and in the appropriateness of leadership style. Emergency conditions do not permit time for deliberation, so that directive styles become necessary under these conditions. Military operations, law enforcement, and fire fighting furnish examples of need for directive leadership. When more time is available for deliberation, as in solving a research problem, the leadership style can be participative.

Rapidity of change and turbulence in the environment affect other aspects of leadership style. Directive styles are normally associated with centralized, formalized organization structure. Under those conditions organizations are more rigid and resistant to change. More open organizations headed by participative leaders are more adaptive to external forces. Lawrence and Lorsch concluded from their studies that "classical theory tends to hold in more stable environments, while the human relations theory is more appropriate to dynamic situations." [4]

Examples of the effect of external variables on leadership style and the qualifications of leaders are almost without end. Successful labor and union relations require certain types of leaders depending on such situational factors as union strength and militancy. Firms that do business with the government are inclined to hire as leaders former military officers or government employees, who know the workings of government agencies and have influence through the friends they left behind. Industries that depend in some way on complicated technology reserve many of their key leadership positions solely for the technocrat; in aerospace, for example, practically all program managers must have a technical background.

Cultural forces also affect leadership, as the pressure for more women in leadership positions attests. Earlier there was a change in cultural attitude toward authority and a demand for increased permissiveness, especially among the younger employees. As a reaction to what John W. Gardner calls the antileader vaccine, some elements of our populace are not seeking leadership positions at all; they associate them with compromise, corruption, and goals that are antithetical to society's best interests.

APPLICATION OF THE SITUATIONAL MODEL

Granted that internal and external variables affect the need for and success of different leadership styles, how is that represented in the situational model? Of what use is the continuum concept in representing the relationships? Figure 8 answers those questions. The leadership continuum, the top line, is the dependent variable. Next come five of the most significant dimensions of situations, the independent variables. If tasks are highly routine, other things being equal, directive leadership is called for; and that is indicated by the first dashed line at the left. The next horizontal line is the technology continuum. As indicated earlier, diverse, problem-solving tasks normally call for participative leadership, and that is what the dashed line from the technology continuum indicates.

Figure 8. **Situational analysis of leadership.**

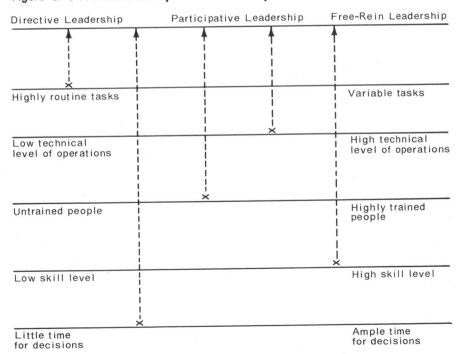

As shown by the third dashed line, a moderate degree of training calls for participative leadership. A high level of skill, however, calls for free-rein leadership, as shown by the dashed line from the skill continuum. The final dimension is the time available for decision making. When there is little time directive leadership is necessary.

The five dimensions in Figure 8 call for a broad range of leadership style. They are not intended to represent one situation; instead, they furnish a variety of examples for illustrative purposes. In practice, however, the various dimensions can be expected to fall within a fairly narrow band on the leadership continuum. Highly repetitive tasks are typically low in technology and also low in the skill and training requirements of people. All three dimensions would call for directive leadership. Professional tasks are normally high in technology, low in routine, and high in skill and training dimensions, all of which point to the selection of participative or free-rein leaders.

However, it should not be assumed from Figure 8 and its analysis that dimensions can be so precisely measured that leadership style can be specified exactly. The situational analysis chart is valuable for its general relationships and not for the specific quantifications. For educational and training purposes information can be more easily communicated and understood if it is shown schematically. Also, those relationships are much easier to appreciate. The situational analysis chart, then, is intended to show the relationship of situational variables to leadership styles, and it is extremely revealing in analyzing leadership patterns.

Implications of the Situational Approach

The situational approach to leadership has many implications. The first major one is that a leader should analyze a situation and then pick the leadership style that would be appropriate to it. The assumption is that, as he moves from situation to situation, he can slip along the leadership continuum from free-rein to directive and back to participative style.

However, Fred Fiedler and many other behavioralists would question anyone's flexibility in that regard. They distinguish between leadership style and leadership behavior. Over a long time span leadership style represents the consistent leadership pattern of an individual. Leadership behavior, on the other hand, consists of specific acts over a short term that may deviate from the long-term, generalized pattern.

Leadership styles can be compared with personality characteristics. An individual's personality can be classified in a certain way, and most of his behavior will be consistent with the description. Occasionally, however, deviations such as fits of anger or mood fluctuations will be observed. So it is in leadership. Individuals will tend to display a consistent pattern in leading others, but some of their acts will deviate from the general pattern. From that it can be concluded that the normal individual cannot, day in and day out, fluctuate from one leadership style to another. His perception, personality characteristics, and experience will force him to resort to a specific style. The expectations of others and his perceived role will affect his behavior and the way he leads, but that effect will be relatively consistent as long as he maintains the same position and associates with approximately the same people. That is not to imply that a participative leader should not occasionally be directive or free-rein. It does imply that there is little chance of changing a free-rein leader into a directive one in a short time, if indeed he can be changed at all.

The contingency approach to leadership urges flexibility on the leader, since he will eventually face a variety of situations. However, there are definite psychological limits to the flexibility. A more important effort is to identify the specific instances in which a participative leader should temporarily behave as a directive one or a directive leader behave as a free-rein one. Obviously, the participative leader should employ a directive style during periods of emergency. Also, a free-rein leader should become directive if his group threatens his leadership position and engages in acts contrary to the interests of the organization. It is generally acknowledged that a participative leader should use a directive approach as a last resort in attempting to encourage a subordinate to function at a specific level. If positive approaches to motivation are not successful, it may be necessary to threaten an individual to force him to perform at minimum acceptable levels.

The situational approach to leadership also represents a challenge to some of the most common current techniques of management and leadership training. A significant portion of all management training today is directed at attempting to change the attitudes, openness, or understanding of leadership. Sensitivity training is a prime example. However, we know that attempting to change people psychologically is a very slow and uncertain process. A more productive approach is suggested by situational analysis. Perhaps we should concentrate more on being able to comprehend different situations and to identify the leaders with the particular styles that those situations call for. One of the most important leadership criteria, then, should be the particular style the individual normally displays. The selection process is then a matter of matching the leadership demands of the situation with the leadership styles represented by the potential candidates.

A companion point of significance is that it is probably easier to change situations than people. Of all the factors in the situation, the basic motivational need structures of people are probably the most difficult to modify. It is often considerably easier to change the tasks performed, the organizational structure, or the manner in which technology is utilized. The change process in organizations must concentrate on all those factors, and not just on the people factor. As Professor J. Sterling Livingston of Harvard University says, "It is a serious mistake to teach managers that they should adopt styles that are artificial and inconsistent with their unique personalities. Yet this is precisely what a large number of business organizations are doing, and it explains, in part, why their management development programs are not effective." [5]

A final implication of situational analysis as it relates to leadership is that an organization should avoid inbreeding. All organizations require a variety of leadership styles and capabilities to meet a variety of situations. In this chapter we have focused on leadership styles associated with the use of authority, but other characteristics are also important. Some situations call for leaders who are outstanding planners; some for leaders who are expert organizers; and some for leaders who are specialists in control. An organization must have a leadership repertoire to meet its many needs.

ten
situational factors in motivation

TO RELATE situational analysis to all management functions and activities is not possible in this book, but the appropriateness of situational analysis to some of the key aspects of management and supervision can be demonstrated. Leadership style having been considered in Chapter 9, situational analysis will be applied to motivation, a closely related behavioral consideration, in this chapter.

Our knowledge of human motivation is as restricted as our overall knowledge of human behavior. Currently we know few absolute answers, nor have we any simple theory or a set of guidelines in lieu of one. Research results are often conflicting, so there are many different theories. Fortunately, however, there is some agreement about the basic nature of drives and motives.

The first distinction of importance is that between motivation and behavior. Motives are internal wants or needs that result in drives and ultimately in behavior: The wants create tensions that cause the individual to behave in a certain way to relieve them, or to obtain specific need satisfaction. Wants are called socially conditioned needs because their intensity and degree of satisfaction are determined through interaction with others. Motives are the whys of behavior. They get at the source of human activity and the peculiarities of behavior. They deal with the internal drives that energize and direct behavior, and yet motivation is not strictly an internal condition. Needs, drives, and behavior are goal-oriented. They are directed at achieving external goals or conditions that are a form of need satisfaction. Thus drive is internal but behavior as such is externally directed at goals.

Motives are only one aspect of behavior. To explain all the behavior of an individual would require consideration of more than just the needs or wants that stimulate action. Personal behavior is affected by those basic wants, but it is also a function of such factors as prior experience, frame of reference, attitudes, norms of the groups with which the individual identifies, and the expectations of others. Behavior is a composite of many factors associated with the individual's perception, environment, and physical and mental capabilities. In this chapter, however, only the internal motives that result from basic needs or wants will be considered.

MOTIVATION IN MANAGEMENT

From the preceding paragraphs it is apparent that management is concerned with motivation because it involves the enthusiasm and drive of people in work situations. One of the prime responsibilities of leadership is to motivate the members in an organization to achieve the goals of the organization. Thus, leaders must understand the nature of needs and wants if they are to influence human behavior.

The theoretical structure that will be used to analyze needs is Maslow's needs hierarchy. It is used for two reasons. First, even though it was one of the earliest theories of motivation, it continues to be widely used, and it has served as a takeoff point for essentially all subsequent theories. The more recent theories of behaviorialists—those of McGregor, Herzberg, Likert, and Vroom, for example—are based on the Maslow approach. Second, of all the theories on motivation, Maslow's needs construct is probably the most understandable and utilitarian for both the academician and the practitioner. Although broad in scope, it has a practicality that gives it strong appeal. It is not, however, beyond criticism. The validity of any theory that purports to compartmentalize and structure sources of behavior is challenged at once by the capricious nature of behavior. Examples of exceptions to the categorizations are all too easy to enumerate.

Abraham Maslow, an American psychologist, first presented his needs hierarchy in 1943. Psychologists had long recognized that such needs as recognition, acceptance, and security affect behavior. However, Maslow grouped all the needs into a five-step hierarchy and made specific assumptions about needs at the different levels of the hierarchy:

1. *Physiological needs*—food, clothing, shelter, and other needs that have to do with man's physical well-being.

2. *Security and safety needs* also deal primarily with man's physical well-being. They involve being safe from tyranny, assault, temperature extremes, physical dangers, and so on.

3. *Social or love needs* are the first of the higher or psychological needs and come from the individual's desire to have others accept him. The basic need is for a sense of belonging and involvement. Man is a social animal, and the opportunity to interact and gain the acceptance of others is basic to his motivation.

4. *Esteem or ego needs*. In his interaction with others man also seeks recognition. Basic to the behavior of human beings is the need to feel competent. Most people seek independence and achievement opportunities that, when successfully handled, provide a feeling of adequacy and self-esteem. Man's behavior in organizations is frequently dictated by ego needs.

5. *Self-actualization needs* are difficult to distinguish from the esteem or ego needs. Self-actualization is the internal desire for self-fulfillment; it is the individual's desire to realize his potential. The need is obviously never fully realized, but its partial realization results in feelings of self-worth and achievement associated with ego needs. It is a basic internal drive, largely unfulfilled, that characterizes man as a wanting animal.

Maslow considered the five needs to be the basic motivators of human behavior. However, his important contribution was not in the identification of needs, but in his belief that a satisfied need is not a motivator. Also, he believed that the potency of needs depends on the degree of need satisfaction consistent with the hierarchy shown in Figure 9. Needs of the lowest level, physiological needs, will take priority over other needs until they are satisfied at minimum acceptable levels. After they are satisfied, higher-level needs become predominant. The need to have water will completely dominate the behavior of a man who is dying of thirst, but it will not greatly influence the immediate behavior of someone who has recently consumed a large volume of this liquid. Since a want ceases to be a motivator once it is satisfied, Maslow considered physiological needs to be relatively unimportant in our society. Granted that poverty is still with us, few people experience sustained periods of extreme hunger or deprivation of other physical requirements.

The next most important needs are those on the step immediately above physiological needs in the hierarchy: safety and security needs. Accordingly, once physiological needs are satisfied, they take over as the basic motivators. However, Maslow felt that, under normal conditions, they too are fulfilled, so that in today's society they are not important factors in behavior. He therefore concluded that the psychological needs that have to do with acceptance, esteem, and self-actualization are the least fulfilled and therefore the strongest determinants of behavior. Regarding those needs the hierarchy concept is significant. Social needs are generally the most fulfilled, and self-actualization is generally the least fulfilled. The hierarchy therefore accurately represents the strength of the needs as resulting from their degree of satisfaction.

Figure 9. Maslow's hierarchy of human needs.

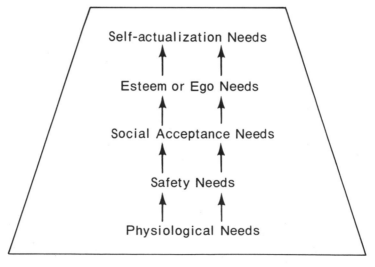

The structure of Maslow's needs hierarchy is simple, but the interpretation of it is complex. No two people have needs of equal intensity, nor are the needs equally satisfied. For those reasons, individuals will not respond to opportunities for need satisfaction in the same way. Needs are affected by experience, and, as Maslow himself indicates, individuals have personal hierarchies that are contrary to the structure he proposed. To some people, as an example, recognition is less important than a need for social acceptance, even assuming that both needs are equally satisfied. Needs are also affected by aspiration levels, values, personal expectations, and many other factors. However, Maslow's hierarchy is still a useful, generalized approach to the interpretation of human motives and the attempt to evaluate incentive systems in industry.

Applying Motivational Theory

Maslow's needs hierarchy contributes to an understanding of motives and the basic rewards people strive for in the work situation. A reasonable conclusion from Maslow's construction is that the worker intends, by his behavior, to gain need satisfaction in the form of acceptance by others, recognition from others, and a feeling of achievement and competency from the tasks performed. However, that again is too simplified if it is necessary to assume that management's job is simply that of giving people a feeling of recognition and achievement for what they do. There are always competing sources of need satisfaction. A worker might get recognition from the work group by thwarting what the supervisor wants done if the informal group norm is inconsistent with the formal work standards. Also, the basic satisfaction of many workers' psychological needs comes from activities off the job, not on it. The job is simply a way to acquire the financial means of pursuing avocational interests.

Many have concluded that Maslow considered money to be unimportant as an incentive because it is related to physiological needs that are themselves not important as motivators. However, money can satisfy many needs depending on its utilization. Certainly it can provide a sense of satisfaction and be a way of changing social relationships, as by membership in a country club, and it is widely recognized in our culture as a symbol of status and power. It can even relate to self-actualization if it affords someone the free time to pursue self-fulfillment drives.

If an organization has a morale problem and the members of the group appear to lack motivation, the supervisor might profitably use an analytical framework based on needs. Basically, there are only two reasons for lack of motivation and incompetence: the individual and the organization. Too often we are inclined to attribute lack of productivity entirely to the individual. The trouble may indeed be the individual if he lacks the skills, attitudes, training, work habits, personality, or drive necessary to function effectively in his job. But poor performance and low morale can also be due to the organizational climate. Ineffective leaders, poorly designed jobs, inequitable pay and fringe benefits, lack of opportunity for advancement, ill-conceived rules and regulations, and disruptive social relationships can discourage people who have adequate skills and a proper mental outlook. Frequently, instead of asking what is wrong with the worker, we should ask what is wrong with the work we require him to perform. Needs are strong motivators only when the opportunities for their fulfillment are rewarding and realistic to the individual.

SITUATIONAL ANALYSIS AND THE NEEDS THEORY

On the assumption that needs are important sources of motivation, need theory will be applied to the factors and dimensions in the situational model of management. The attempt, as in Chapter 9, is to demonstrate the usefulness of the model in approaching such management problems as motivation. The attempt is rather limited because it is confined to elementary need theory as it is related to motivation. Also, there is little documentation of the observations made; in fact, many of the observations consist essentially of restatements of concepts presented earlier in the book. The methodology is the same as in Chapter 9: each factor in the contingency model will be presented along with factor dimensions that are significant in motivation.

The Purpose Factor and Motivation

The purpose factor is critical to motivation because an individual's commitment to the tasks of the organization is closely related to how he identifies with the organization purpose. If he has values, interests, and needs that are consistent with the organization's values, interests, and needs, then he succeeds when the organization succeeds. Certain programs tend to be much more psychologically attractive than others, however. Those related to the national interest, such as the race to the moon, scientific breakthroughs, such as cancer research, and social benefits, such as orphan adoption centers, are examples. But when a worker is engaged in unskilled physical tasks involving a product that has no significance to him, that kind of commitment is more difficult to obtain.

Management-by-objectives programs are deliberate attempts to establish a process of organizational and personal goal setting. The intent is to integrate the goals of the various elements of the organization and focus attention and effort on the primary activities involved in goal accomplishment.

The purpose factor has special significance for the management process of employee selection and training. Whenever possible, employees who have values, interests, and abilities consistent with the values, interests, and abilities implied in the institutional purpose should be selected.

The Task Factor and Motivation

Perhaps the most basic concept in motivation today is that for an individual to be highly motivated in performing his job he must be engaged in tasks that give him feelings of recognition and accomplishment. In the work situation the desire for a feeling of competence can best be satisfied through tasks that provide outlets for skill utilization, afford some independence, and are sufficiently complex to provide a feeling of esteem.

Many of the task dimensions can be directly related to opportunities for need satisfaction. Repetitive, specialized tasks that demand little skill, as in routine production, provide little opportunity for the satisfaction of ego or self-actualization needs. Thus many of the present-day motivational programs are directed at enlarging or enriching jobs to make them more demanding, more challenging, and less routine. An attempt is also made to increase the range of the job cycle so that the employee completes a larger portion of the total task sequence. That gives him a greater feeling of accomplishment and increases his sense of responsibility for the end item.

Other dimensions of the task factor have similar effects on motivation. Tasks with high sequential independence often call for people with high affiliation as opposed to achievement needs. The structure of the assembly line masks individualized effort and leaves little room for a feeling of achievement. Also, tasks that are high on the working-with-people dimension call for individuals who display strong social needs. The other parallels are obvious. Independent tasks require people who have a need for independence; tasks that require superior reasoning skills or mathematical skills should be handled by people with those capabilities who can get a feeling of achievement from what they do. On the other hand, it is often difficult for an individual with strong ego needs to fill a staff position in which he should remain in the background to be effective.

The most important managerial problem in motivation is twofold: Management must, when possible, design jobs that include tasks and goals of interest to employees, and it should select employees who can successfully accomplish the tasks. If the tasks are challenging enough that the employee who successfully handles them gets a feeling of achievement, they will tend to be motivational. There are, of course, problems in all this. Many tasks are by nature simple and routine, and opportunities for job enlargement simply do not exist. Also, what is challenging to one individual may not be challenging to another. The problem of relating people with different needs to different tasks in different situations remains.

The Technology Factor and Motivation

The technical content of the methods and operations of an organization has been found to be one of the situational dimensions that influences the motivation of subordinates. Technical and scientific operations involve varied, problem-solving, complex tasks that frequently offer ample opportunity for recognition and self-actualization need satisfaction, assuming the individual has the necessary capability. The independence and challenge offered by research problems can be enough to stimulate scientists to be interested in their work and so require little formal direction.

However, status and recognition are relative. If a scientist is much less successful than his peers in making discoveries and solving problems, he is deprived of recognition and frustrated in his work. Gaining esteem is not simply a matter of success in accomplishing specific tasks or of the relationship between individuals and tasks. Esteem is a function of how successful others are in performing similar tasks, and it is a function of how successful the individual expects to be in performing those tasks. If he is only moderately successful but expected to be highly successful, he might be discouraged rather than stimulated by the experience.

In general, however, the basic principle of motivation holds. Operations that are low in technology are typically simple and routine. They demand that the individual do little more than perform a shallow set of physical motions, but they also reward him in a very limited way—they give him little psychological need satisfaction. More complex technical or scientific operations are both more demanding of skills and more rewarding in satisfaction of ego and achievement needs.

Not all dimensions with a high technical input necessarily have a positive effect on motivation. Automation is a good example. A craftsman might be highly motivated because of his ability in utilizing his skills. A carpenter or pipe fitter can gain a feeling of pride and achievement from his work if he applies his craft in a way that gains him recognition—his is the same pride-of-ownership feeling that is fundamental to participative management. Sometimes craft work is superseded by automation and a skilled machinist is given the job of monitoring and maintaining the equipment. He can no longer identify with the end product because it does not represent his skills. Automation, an important measure of technology, often makes jobs less motivational because the worker finds it so difficult to associate his efforts with any specific, identifiable achievements.

Machinery and automation have many other effects on motivation.

Machines often dictate the pace at which the individual works and force him to perform his work in a fixed location. Each constraint affects social needs, independence needs, and feelings of achievement.

Science and technology are often accompanied by physical side effects such as heat, cold, eyestrain, and muscular fatigue. Employees experience eyestrain when they scan, for eight hours a day, the photographs from hydrogen bubble chamber experiments. A food processor moving into the frozen food line will find it difficult to entice his employees into working in cold storage warehouses in which the temperature remains at zero. Technology that has a negative influence on the physical environment will, in that way, have a negative influence on morale.

The People Factor and Motivation

In a study of motivation, people are the dependent variable; our question is how the other variables in the situational model affect motivation. As indicated earlier, the results are not consistent because the intensity of needs varies with people. Also, different experiences and expectations make the question of need satisfaction one that can be viewed only in relative terms.

Need satisfaction also tends to advance in ascending cycles. To a business student majoring in accounting, becoming a junior accountant may be a highly motivational goal. Accomplishment of the goal may also provide him with esteem and achievement need satisfaction. In time, however, a new goal replaces the old one. He seeks to be an accountant, then a senior accountant, then a supervisor, and eventually a controller.

Each new goal brings with it opportunities for recognition and advancement. The position of junior accountant was once a highly motivational goal and rewarding in terms of achievement. But if four years later the junior accountant has made no progress on his career ladder, he is deprived of self-esteem and no longer has a feeling of accomplishment. He may be negatively reinforced to the point where he is discouraged about his career.

People are the most complex and least understood of all internal factors in the situational model, so that establishing dependent relationships between the other factors and the people factor is difficult and often borders on speculation. However, those relationships are an advance over the carrot-and-stick rules of thumb about motivation that have served many managers in the past.

In considering the people factor, one of the most important aspects is the influence that other people have on the individual. Role expectations, organization standards, and social relationships exert influence on need formulation and satisfaction. Affiliation, ego, and self-actualization needs are socially conditioned and are satisfied only on the basis of social relationships. Thus the people-to-people dimensional interface is probably more important than the people-to-task, people-to-technology, or people-to-structure interfaces.

The Structure Factor and Motivation

The many different dimensions of structure lead to many possible separate analyses of structure and its relation to motivation. Fortunately, several of the structural dimensions result in conditions that have a similar effect on motivation, which permits the dimensions to be grouped. Highly formalized, bureaucratic structures with detailed job specifications tend to be very restrictive. Rules and regulations cover most activities, and the atmosphere encourages conformity and discourages creative approaches. Since a worker has little control over his activities and experiences limited independence, it is difficult for him to feel that he is contributing to the level of his potential.

Opportunities for recognition and self-actualization are more restricted in formalized than in more open organizations. The formalized organization is also normally characterized by centralization of authority. The same pattern of need satisfaction tends to follow, with the employee making few decisions, having little responsibility, and feeling his ideas and capabilities are underutilized. Under reverse conditions, in which the situation structure is less formalized and authority is decentralized, the individual freedom of action provided results in much more opportunity for psychological need satisfaction.

The size of the organization is an important factor in motivation associated primarily with social and ego need satisfaction. Small groups are conducive to people developing more intimate relationships and gaining a stronger feeling of acceptance and belonging that are extremely difficult to attain in large organizations. As a result, large organizations in time become a conglomeration of many smaller ones. The freshman student at a large university feels no sense of belonging and is, in fact, little more than a number until he identifies with campus subgroups.

Span of control is also affected by the size of the groups in an organization. The effects are the same as those of size except for one important difference. Subordinates do not like large spans of control if the supervisor has so many subordinates that he cannot be sufficiently familiar with the work of any of them to know when an outstanding job is being done. In the business organization, in which the reward system is tied to pleasing the supervisor, gaining the confidence and approval of a superior is a vital factor in ego need satisfaction.

The emphasis in business firms on the concept of hierarchy places a premium on attaining higher levels in the chain of command. Both recognition and power come from climbing upward in the organization, which makes the hierarchy a significant factor in assessing motivation and need satisfaction. This is an example of a socially conditioned need: symbols of authority and power represented by positions at the different levels of the hierarchy affect the aspirations and feelings of accomplishment of individuals.

Many other aspects of formal organization structure can be related to motivation. As indicated earlier, the motivational effect of line or staff positions depends on individual needs and temperaments. Cohesive groups obviously offer more security and belonging need satisfaction to their members and will be motivational to individuals for whom those needs are intense. On the other hand, a stable organization may frustrate people with high esteem and self-actualization needs. If the stable organization offers little opportunity for promotion or advancement, the striving, competent employee, who otherwise would be one of the most enthusiastic individuals in the work group, is apt to be discouraged.

Most of the statements that have been made about the formal organization structure as it affects motivation are true of the informal structure also. Informal organization structure can provide opportunities for power, recognition, belonging, and self-actualization just the same as formal structure can. One of the strengths of informal structure is that the worker can get a feeling of acceptance from it that he cannot get from the more formal structure. Also, many individuals are strongly identified with the informal structure because their positions as informal leaders provide them with need satisfaction that they cannot attain in the formal organization. The strength of the informal structure derives from its capability for providing certain need satisfactions that cannot be obtained or that are attainable only to a more limited degree in the formal structure.

Environmental Factors and Motivation

Environmental factors have a more direct influence on the total organization than on individuals within the organization. Thus the motivational impact of environmental factors is dependent in part upon the degree to which the individual identifies with the broader organization. A common enemy or external threat can consolidate an organization and affect individual security and belonging needs. If the organization is successful in competing with other firms and the individual identifies with the organization, he can equate that success with his own.

Some external variables do directly affect the individual, however. Changing technology can exert pressures on the organization, so that individuals with appropriate technical skills become more important to

153

the organization. That opens up opportunities for those individuals and can give them greater feelings of self-esteem and accomplishment. In contrast, certain requirements of governments, especially reporting requirements, may make some jobs more tedious and serve as irritants. External economic conditions may stop the growth of an organization, which will reduce the opportunities to the individual and thus affect his security and accomplishment need satisfaction.

Since needs are socially conditioned, some of the important factors in need formulation and satisfaction are customs and the behavioral demands of a society. David C. McClelland argues that there are substantial differences in need achievement among cultures. He traces the industrial growth of nations to the changes in achievement motivation. He sees achievement needs as the central issue in developing nations and in international competition. He concludes:

> So the question of what happens to our civilization or to our business community depends quite literally on how much time tens of thousands or even millions of us spend thinking about achievement, about setting moderate achievable goals, taking calculated risks, assuming personal responsibility, and finding out how well we have done our job.[1]

The importance of the Puritan work ethic in the early development of the United States is a good example of cultural norms affecting motivation.

Maslow's need hierarchy is utilized in this chapter as an example of how an analysis of motivation can be based on the situational model of management. Although Maslow's theory is not complete or even totally accurate, it is the source of most other theories and it also has considerable practical utility. By applying it to the contingency model, the value of situational analysis can be demonstrated. Motivation is not simply a relationship between an individual and the tasks he performs, as many writers would lead us to believe. Motivation is affected by that relationship, but it is also affected by purpose, technology, structure, and such external factors as culture, technology, government, and economic conditions.

Situational analysis forces a much broader, more thorough consideration of management problems than techniques utilized in the past. Further, it warns that there is no one best way to motivate just as there is no one best way to lead or organize. Motivation is a function of many factors in situations, and any course of action to improve motivation can be determined only after a proper consideration of the variables involved. Motivation is both situationally determined and situationally influenced, which should encourage managers to use a situational framework for analytical purposes.

eleven
planning, control, and financial systems

IN EARLIER CHAPTERS situational analysis has been applied primarily to behavioral considerations involving leadership, motivation, and organization concepts. In this chapter the versatility of situational analysis will be demonstrated by applying it to the essentially nonbehavioral considerations of business systems. "Business systems," as used here, are those established to allocate, schedule, and account for resources and their utilization. The selection of business systems should be based on situational analysis just as leadership style and organization should be. Different business systems are established to meet different needs. A mismatch between specific systems and conditions within an organization can prove disastrous to planning, controlling, and reporting.

Situational differences are as evident in business systems as in any other area of management activity. There are no principles of planning that apply to all organizations, just as there are no across-the-board predictors of human behavior. There is no one best accounting system or planning format. There may be one best system for a particular firm at a particular time, but systems cannot be lifted intact from one organization and applied with equal effectiveness to another. Furthermore, since organizations are changing, dynamic entities, the one best plan or system for a company today may not be the one best plan or system tomorrow when the characteristics of the situation have changed.

Many of the situational differences in planning are obvious. Diverse firms will necessarily adopt dissimilar strategies and objectives in their long-range planning. Differences in resources, processes, and products will also necessitate different controls and emphasis in scheduling. The depth and the detail of planning will vary in accordance with such dimensions as size, operations, and conditions of uncertainty. The participation of employees in the planning process will depend upon the needs of the organization and the competence and background of the employees. The manager's challenge is, again, to select from the vast array of available business systems and concepts those that will be the most effective in the particular environment in which he finds himself.

In order to pinpoint the influence of situational factors on the selection and effectiveness of business systems and concepts, the method of the preceding two chapters will be followed. Each of the major factors in the situational model will be reviewed to determine the effect it has on the need for specific business systems and concepts. To keep the analysis relatively simple, five planning and scheduling and four budget and accounting systems will be considered. The nine systems were chosen because they represent the basic systems in essentially all industrial organizations. Furthermore, the effectiveness of each depends on a specific set of conditions within a company. The systems are included also because their wide utilization will increase reader familiarization with the examples presented. The systems included in this analysis are as follows:

Planning and scheduling systems: Gantt charts, milestone charts, network analysis (PERT, CMP, and so on), flow control scheduling, programmed scheduling.

Budget and accounting systems: fixed budgets, variable or flexible budgets, standard cost systems, actual cost systems.

A glossary of terms is provided at the end of this chapter for readers who are not familiar with the systems to be discussed.

PLANNING SYSTEMS

Planning systems are divided into two basic types: strategic or long-range and operational or short-range. Strategic plans deal primarily with the external factors in the situational model; they are an exercise in situational analysis. A firm attempts to look into the future as far as the long-range timetable established; it attempts to determine how the external environment will change in that time period. If the plan is for five years, the concern is how technological, political, social, and economic forces will change in that time and what their relative importance will be. Before a firm can establish strategies or goals, it must evaluate competitors and the conditions that will exist in the period specified. They are the dominating factors that will determine if goals are realistic or unrealistic and if they reflect the milieu of the situation. Future goals are meaningful only if a reasonably accurate prediction is made of the environment that will exist when goal accomplishment is to take place.

Short-range or operational plans relate primarily to the conditions internal to the firm. The typical effort is to schedule resources and processes to optimize internal operating efficiency. All nine of the specified business systems are intended primarily to meet internal needs. The analysis is therefore divided into two parts. The five internal factors—purpose, tasks, technology, people, and structure—will be related to the nine systems. The five external factors—technology, governments, law, social forces, and economic forces—will be related to broader planning considerations such as planning strategies. The discussion of external systems will be much more abbreviated, since the systems that exist for long-range planning are less formalized.

SITUATIONAL ANALYSIS OF BUSINESS SYSTEMS

Several dimensions of internal factors tend to dictate the need for certain types of business systems. Since scheduling and financial systems are to account for and control operations, it follows that the tasks that compose the operations dominate other considerations. However, technology is often paramount, especially if it determines the nature of the tasks. Table 5 relates a few of the key situational dimensions to the need for specific types of planning, scheduling, budgeting, and accounting systems. The table does not include all dimensions that influence the effectiveness of specific business systems; it includes only those that tend to prevail in the typical industrial firm. The impact of each dimension will be discussed in relation to the primary factor with which it is associated.

The Purpose Factor and Business Systems

As indicated earlier, the basic tasks involved in the operations of an organization are the prime determinant of the business systems required. Accordingly, the purpose of the organization has a major indirect influence on business systems—the purpose determines the tasks. A large firm that is intended to make a profit through the production of goods will

Table 5. Situational analysis of business system application.

Factor	Dimension	Evaluation	Gantt Chart	Milestone Chart	Network (PERT)	Flow Control	Programmed Scheduling	Fixed Budget	Variable Budget	Standard Cost	Actual Cost
			Planning and Scheduling					Budget and Accounting			
Task	Repetition	High				x	x		x	x	
		Low	x	x	x						x
	Time range	Short				x	x		x	x	
		Long	x	x	x						x
	Throughput	Low	x	x	x						x
		High				x	x		x	x	
	Functional nature	Prod'n				x	x		x	x	
		R&D	x	x	x			x			x
Technology	Technical content of operations	High	x	x	x			x			x
		Low				x	x		x	x	
	Automation	High				x	x		x	x	
		Low	x	x	x						x
External	Technological change	Slow				x	x		x	x	
		Rapid	x	x	x						x

use detailed, sophisticated systems for planning, scheduling, and accounting because the output, by its physical nature, is measurable in units produced and input resources required. Physical production counts provide discrete information that can be analyzed and utilized in many ways.

The production firm can be contrasted with an organization with goals that are social in nature and involve a service. Under those circumstances systems for planning, evaluating, and accounting are restricted because so little is measurable in either units or results. In most instances quantifiable, social standards as a basis for evaluating performance do not exist. It is obviously easier and more appropriate to utilize detailed variable budgets, programmed scheduling, and standard cost systems in organizations that have economic and utilitarian purposes and produce goods for consumption in the marketplace than it is to use such systems in organizations with goals that are ethical, political, or social in nature.

The Task Factor and Business Systems

The nature of the tasks performed in an organization dominates all other considerations in the selection of business systems, and the most important task dimensions are repetition, sequential interdependence, and throughput rate. By those three dimensions manufacturing is divided into two basic types: intermittent production and continuous production. They can be contrasted with R&D, in which there is no repetition in production. Research and development, intermittent production, and continuous production will be used to explore the need for different business systems as determined by task dimensions.

Research and development. The unique features of R&D have already been described. An R&D project is at the extreme left end of the repetition continuum. By definition R&D encompasses experimental activities in which no repetition in operations is involved. R&D is also at the low point on the throughput rate continuum because only a few experimental units are produced. Under those circumstances Gantt charts, milestone charts, and network models such as PERT are applicable. Those planning systems are useful when the specific resources required, the time constraints of the operations, and the performance outcomes involve many unknowns.

In R&D the goal is to discover knowledge, establish processes, or design a product that currently does not exist. Accordingly time, cost, and performance are not known and can only be approximated. Managerial decision making in relation to R&D is dependent upon an awareness of the cost incurred, the projected dates for the work to be accomplished, and the performance achieved versus the goals of the project. Those

159

factors are emphasized in systems utilizing Gantt charts, milestone charts, and PERT networks.

The misapplication of PERT offers a strong argument for situational analysis; it has also tended to undermine the utility of both PERT and similar management systems. PERT was widely acclaimed as an effective planning and control device after its successful use in development of the Polaris missile system. The Navy Department felt that it helped speed up the schedule by as much as two years. In the 1960s, after PERT's success was widely publicized, many organizations adopted the technique as a scheduling panacea. Also, the Department of Defense enthusiasm resulted in essentially all large industrial R&D contractors being required to use network analysis.

In all this jubilation the essential limitations of PERT were ignored. PERT was designed to apply in specific situations that are referred to as one-of-a-kind single-use projects. In such situations a set of operations is performed in a particular sequence for the very first time, such as one finds in R&D or in the construction of major buildings. PERT was not intended for and has little value in situations in which costs and scheduling requirements are known because operations have already been performed many times in an established sequence. In other PERT misapplications planners were required to conduct in-depth planning involving thousands of events scheduled many weeks in the future when the uncertainties of state of the art research made such detailed planning an exercise in intuition bordering on futility. As a result of its misapplications, PERT soon lost much of its glamour. Today it is probably ignored by organizations that could benefit from its use.

The PERT example provides one of the most important lessons of situational analysis. When a manager utilizes a planning and control system or any similar technique, two things are important: he must understand the system or concept, and he must also understand the conditions to which it applies. Too often students and managers gain an understanding of a management tool such as PERT but do not sufficiently appreciate the situational differences that make use of the tool appropriate or inappropriate. Organizations invest heavily in business systems, computers, and management aids that all too often are inefficiently used because management does not know when and how they should be used.

As for budget and accounting systems, it is normally mandatory that R&D organizations adopt fixed budgets and actual cost systems. Cost standards can be determined only after cost experience has been gained by repetitively producing an item the specifications of which remain constant. A variable budget requires that either costs or conditions be standard so that the budget can be related to activity levels, not time periods. Since R&D does not meet that requirement, the less desirable fixed budget based on actual cost systems is normally used.

Business systems in intermittent production. A job shop is an example of intermittent production that, in respect to the dimensions or characteristics of the tasks involved, is halfway between R&D and continuous production. In a job shop a variety of small jobs are custom-fabricated to order. The jobs are characterized by low repetition and volume. All the machining operations are similar but their sequencing is different, as one would expect when projects are varied and each job is fabricated to meet a customer's requirements.

That each job is normally different results in order control. Each order must be individually estimated, routed, time-sequenced, budgeted, and regulated. Gantt charts are ideal for the purpose because they show the sequencing of operations and the associated time constraints. Operations sheets are also used to specify the type and order of the processes. The accounting system utilized is by definition job order. Lack of repetition in the operations means that an actual- rather than a standard-cost system is normally appropriate.

Systems for continuous production. In contrast with the job shop and R&D, mass production is characterized by high repetition, high sequential interdependence, and large volume or throughput rate. Because of the repetitive nature of the assembly line, on which information has been accumulated from continuous production runs, the unknowns of R&D now become knowns. Quality standards are established; time factors are known; and unit costs are a matter of record. Since all of the planning parameters are essentially indisputable, there is no need for Gantt or milestone charts or PERT networks in the planning and monitoring of projects.

In a high-volume assembly line operation the scheduling problem is that of matching the rates of flow of parts and subassemblies with the rate of the main assembly. The inputs must flow in an integrated fashion through the various work stations until the final product is completely assembled. Other controls on the flow of parts are colors, models, and accessories. The timing and cost of the individual operations are standardized, so that scheduling and budgeting can be automatically programmed. Standard cost systems and variable budgets become extremely effective tools for controlling operations. Labor and material utilization can be measured against standards that are both reliable and valid. Given all of these knowns, cost control becomes much more detailed and effective. When standards to measure time, cost, and performance considerations are available, decision making is improved and an extremely accurate picture of the current status of an organization's operations is provided.

Research and development, intermittent production, and continuous production provide important contrasts in industrial organizations. Each is characterized by different points on the repetition, sequential interdependence, and throughput rate continuums. Each lends itself to different planning, scheduling, budgeting, and accounting systems primarily because of a difference in availability of information on time, cost, and performance standards of the tasks involved. Different circumstances or situations that arise from the uniqueness of organizations call for planning, scheduling, budgeting, and accounting systems appropriate to the uniqueness. However, the uniqueness that is more apparent than real can be minimized by a comparison of one situation with another on a basis of common factors and dimensions.

Other task dimensions. The time range or job cycle is an important dimension related to business systems. The time range of many missile systems involves a life cycle of ten years or more. Several years are consumed in research, development, and test programs before the first standardized unit is produced. In the Apollo program billions of dollars were expended for the first successful moon landing. Under those circumstances planning and control systems such as milestone charts and PERT networks are appropriate. From a budget and accounting standpoint, fixed budgets and actual cost systems are normally the most useful. The contrast is with tasks that feature job cycles measured in minutes or hours. In repetition of that type, flow control, standard costs, and variable budgets are appropriate.

Other task dimensions that have implications for business system selection are those involving people and things. Working with things implies production tasks that, because of their measurability, permit utilization of the more detailed systems. Working with people implies behavior considerations that are difficult to measure when production counts are unlikely. The vagueness limits the appropriateness of any planning system based on schematic or quantitative data, including production standards or detailed cost accumulations.

Technology and Business Systems

The technical content of operations and methods separates R&D tasks from low-skill ones. Systems and techniques required for technical and scientific research tasks were described in the section on task dimensions. The environment of a research laboratory is far different from that of a retail store or a furniture factory. Uncertainty is a characteristic of almost every aspect of the R&D operation. Problem solving lacks structure. Effort is hard to coordinate; operations are normally not sequenced; and communication outside the inner circle of technicians and scientists is difficult. Lack of cost and time standards force a much more subjective evaluation of progress and performance. Planning is cumbersome and budgeting becomes an exercise in estimating resource requirements over fixed time periods.

Less technical operations of a non-problem-solving nature involve much more certainty. Experience in performing the operations reduces the unknowns and provides historical data on performance standards, cost measurements, and time factors. Here again, the establishment of standards permits programmed scheduling, variable budgets, and standard cost systems.

Methodology and function dimensions. In this analysis the two opposites of R&D and continuous production have been used as examples. However, the technology dimensions of methodology and function have subdivisions that distinguish some of the variations between extremes. By the function dimension, production is said to be unit, batch, or continuous. Each will require a different planning and control system. Differences in research are also noted. Uncertainty is at a maximum in basic research but reduces when the project advances into the applied stages. Each variation has implications for business system selection.

One final point in relation to technology is important. The complexity, uncertainties, and size associated with technological projects have placed demands upon organizations that are of a different magnitude than those associated with the simpler technology of the past. Therefore, it is no surprise that the newer business systems such as network analysis and PERT have developed out of the high-technology programs. Furthermore, it is likely that future innovations in business systems will evolve from operations that are technology-intensive.

People and Business Systems

The people in organizations affect the operation rather than the selection of planning, control, and accounting systems. The training and knowledge of the people who work with various methods will determine how effective those methods are; unless people are trained in the use of a system, the functioning of the system is hampered. Training also influences the degree to which subordinates participate in associated activities such as goal setting. The selection of systems is most affected by the training and knowledge of individuals when changes in systems are contemplated. A firm should be reluctant to adopt a network model such as PERT unless it has trained PERT planning specialists who can handle the technique.

Of the nine business systems considered in this analysis, people affect the operation of budget systems more than any other. Budgets are designed to control costs through people. They are important systems for resource allocation, but they are also evaluation instruments that tend to threaten or reward people depending on performance or results. If budgets become whipping posts for inadequate performance, they create tension, resentment, and even fear in individuals. Often the result is to play the game by keeping costs and performance just at the standards established or to neglect nonmeasurable aspects of performance and concentrate on the measurable aspects related to budget standards.

If individuals feel that budgets are an aid to good management and that the system is their system rather than a control imposed by an outside group, they are more willing to cooperate in making the system effective. However, they can destroy any methodology if that is their will. Finding fault, a lack of willingness to cooperate, and deliberate sabotage can scuttle even the most expertly contrived system. The designers of management systems find that design is the easy part. The hard part is to implement the system when the work force is apprehensive.

Structure and Business Systems

The structure factor is less noted for influencing other factors than it is for being subject to change by those factors. Quite frequently, that is, structure becomes the dependent rather than the independent variable. An example is an organization that decides to institute a long-range planning system and establish a long-range planning staff. If as a result of that decision a long-range planning staff becomes an advisory group to the president, the power structure in the organization could be changed. Similarly, a change from a fixed budget system used primarily for forecasting purposes to a variable budget system that places more power in the hands of cost analysts could change the complexion of the organization. Since planning is one of the primary functions of a manager, any planning system that is an aid in exercising those responsibilities increases the effectiveness and control of supervision.

When structure is the independent variable, it has some direct although limited influences on business systems. Again the size dimension is most important. Organizations with fewer than ten employees have little need for formalized, strategic planning and control systems; but as they become larger and more complex, they are difficult if not impossible to operate effectively without such systems. Small organizations can also get by on simple budgets and accounting systems that provide primarily financial data. Large organizations require managerial accounting systems that cover in detail the operations performed. The size dimension is almost inevitably one of the pivotal dimensions in all management situations.

The influence of the other dimensions of structure is consistent with observations made in earlier chapters. A few examples will suffice. Highly formalized structures are likely to have planning, scheduling, and business systems that reflect that formalization in their detail. Decisions connected with the business systems will be more rapid in decentralized structures with few levels of hierarchy; more organizational levels and greater authority centralization will slow down the systems, especially at the decision points. When the need for the integration of activities is higher than is typical, there is likely to be a greater reliance on planning and scheduling systems. And finally, in the program form of departmentation used in R&D, the planning system based on milestone charts can be expected. Whether these relations are due to structural differences or are merely associated with them is likely to vary with the situation.

Environmental Factors and Business Systems

As was indicated earlier, environmental factors do not normally directly affect internal operating systems with the possible exception of governments, which force business organizations to do much of their accounting for them in regard to income tax withholdings, social security taxes, and corporate income taxes. Also, the turbulence of the external environment affects the stability of internal, operational planning. However, the aspect of planning, scheduling, budgeting, and accounting systems that is most affected by external factors is that of strategic planning in excess of a one-year period. Decisions on plant investment, product lines, production capacity, and technological improvements cannot be made without some idea of what the future may hold.

One of the first steps in establishing a long-range, say, a five-year, plan is to develop planning premises. The premises are the organization's estimates of the conditions that will exist in the projected five-year period; they are intended to answer such questions as the following: Will input resources be available? What will be the status of technology? What personal income will people have to purchase the products the firm offers? Will government involvement be greater? How will the capability of competitors change during the time period? Will the tastes of people change? Will the international market change? Those and many other questions must be answered before a firm can decide how it intends to fit in the markets of the future. That again reflects the organization's need and struggle for adaptation.

In this chapter situational analysis has been extended to cover the need for different business systems. The three typical examples of R&D and intermittent and continuous production have been used to demonstrate the appropriateness of nine separate business systems, five related to planning and scheduling and four to budgeting and accounting. Repetitive, stable operations and tasks are conducive to measurement, so that flow control, programmed scheduling, variable budgets, and standard cost systems are used in connection with them. Nonrepetitive R&D-type tasks require Gantt charts, milestone charts, and network models for planning and scheduling based on fixed budgets and actual costs. Each organization tends to develop systems that are to some degree unique to its own needs and result from the differences in the characteristics of situations.

The contingency approach to management also emphasizes the need to avoid rigidity. Plans can be responsible for rigidities in organizations if managers are reluctant to deviate from them even when changing conditions create opportunities superior to those associated with the original conditions. Situational analysis rejects considerations based on static relationships or absolutes. Instead it emphasizes relativism. No two organizations are the same, although they may have a relative relationship; each organization or situation has different features or dimensions, but again the differences are relative; environmental conditions change from day to day as the result of dynamic external forces, but those differences are also relative. The primary purpose of planning therefore becomes that of adjusting the organization to the continuous changes that characterize its existence.

GLOSSARY OF BUSINESS SYSTEMS TERMS

Actual Cost System   A cost system whereby actual rather than standard or should-be costs are recorded and utilized.

Fixed Budget   A budget that does not adjust to changes from the planned level of activity; it is fixed in relation to the original plan and established periods of time. Also, budgeting at the expected level of activity without adjustment for actual changes in level. Sometimes called appropriation budget because of its use in government. Common in such areas as R&D, in which activity is difficult to measure.

Flow Control   A scheduling technique utilized when resource inputs, manpower inputs, and time increments are known, so that only the flow of the different types of components or parts must be continuously scheduled to regulate day-to-day operations. An example is an automotive assembly line: flow control scheduling coordinates colors and accessories on each automobile.

Gantt Chart   A scheduling technique developed by H. L. Gantt in about 1910. It is a flexible, schematic method based on horizontal and vertical axes used to represent two related sets of information. Normally, time is expressed in a linear fashion horizontally and the work to be done or activities to be performed are listed vertically in the order of their performance. Gantt charts can be used to portray schematically all types of planning information that are time-oriented. The chart is fairly simple and is widely used; many of the more recent scheduling techniques are adaptations of it.

Milestone Chart An adaptation of the Gantt chart that is somewhat more sophisticated. The operations are not simply shown as bars on the time lines; they are subdivided into "milestones" within the programs or major activity phases. A milestone is a discrete event that signals the accomplishment of a significant portion of a program; it marks completion of a goal or task that represents an important point in overall progress. A milestone chart records the sequencing and timing of events from both a planning and control standpoint. For an example see Figure 10(a).

Network Analysis A category of planning techniques in all of which the schedule for a project is shown in network form. Network analysis has had widespread use since the initiation of PERT in 1958. The techniques represent an advance over milestone scheduling because they permit the identification of dependent relationships among events. Time is not shown linearly as on Gantt and milestone charts, but is instead indicated in numerical figures on the lines that represent dependent relationships.

Figure 10. (a) Typical milestone chart; (b) example of a PERT network.

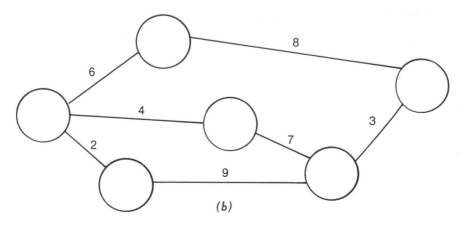

(a)

(b)

Program Evaluation and Review Technique (PERT)   A particular form of network analysis that consists of activities, events, and time estimates. An event, which is represented by a circle in the network, is much the same as a milestone; it marks the completion of a significant phase of the total project. Activity is represented by a line between dependent events; it is the work that must be done to complete an event. The time estimate, the time units necessary to complete an activity, is shown above the activity line. A simple PERT network is shown in Figure 10(*b*). Its virtue lies in its capacity for scheduling both parallel and sequential operations.

Programmed Scheduling   Scheduling in which resource inputs and time factors are so consistent and known that they can be reduced to digital data and processed electronically.

Standard Cost System   A cost system using predetermined costs of manufacturing as the basis for recording costs. A standard represents what the cost of one unit of a product should be under normal operating conditions. Standardized costs are associated with continuous production operations for which there is considerable cost experience. They are extremely useful as a basis for evaluating operations.

Variable Budget   Also called a flexible budget. A budget that adjusts to levels of activity or production; it is normally associated with units of production, not time. Standard costs make variable budgets feasible. If a certain number of units are produced during a given time period, a specific budget is "earned." The basis of earning is the standard cost of the units produced. Variable budgets are also developed by estimating different projected volume levels. The actual budget is then calculated from the estimate that corresponds with the actual volume achieved.

twelve
the new direction of management theory

IF A MIDDLE MANAGER terminates his employment with General Motors and assumes a similar position with Ford, he finds that he has to make only a few changes to adjust to his new position. The people he works with are different and some aspects of the organization structure, such as the details of departmentation, authority delegation, and operating procedures, are different, but much about his job is the same. The purposes of the organizations, the basic operations, and the levels of the technology are essentially identical. Also, since the two corporations have much the same common market, the environments have many similarities. The one notable difference in the environment is the influence of the federal government on each organization. General Motors, with its larger share of the automotive market, is much more subject to action by the Antitrust Division of the Justice Department than is Ford. After four to six months of becoming acquainted with the people and structure variables, the middle manager could function as effectively in his new position as he had in his old one.

If, on the other hand, a middle manager for a firm such as Hercules Powder Company or Thiokol Chemical Corporation transfers from one of the chemical divisions to an aerospace division—even though he remains within the same corporation—he finds the situational differences to be much greater. The people at the corporate headquarters and the overall corporate structure have not changed; the transferee's problem in that regard is to become familiar with the people and organization structure in his new division.

The main changes he faces are in the task, technology, and environmental factors. The operations performed in a chemical plant bear little relationship to the operations of an aerospace plant. Gaining a knowledge of aerospace operations and technology will require a considerably longer adjustment than the four to six months needed by the automotive executive. If the middle manager is engaged in marketing activities, he is likely to need several years rather than several months before he reaches the effectiveness level he achieved in the chemical operations. The government-dominated aerospace market is decidedly different from its commercial chemical counterpart. In marketing, those differences require a complete readjustment of strategies, methods, and success criteria.

In the late 1950s and early 1960s it was commonplace for aerospace firms to transfer in people from other divisions to meet the demands of expanding aerospace operations. Based on the traditional assumption of the universality of management, it was often postulated that only a short period would be required for the transferees to become fully effective in their new positions. But when the differences were as accentuated as those between a chemical and an aerospace division, the companies frequently learned the hard way that the adjustment period stretched out over a

170

prohibitive time span. In many instances the organizations solved the problem by backing up each executive from a different product line with an assistant who had aerospace experience.

Some companies made an even more serious mistake by interpreting R&D instability as mismanagement. They then went to the continuous processing industries such as the automotive firms and hired away middle managers responsible for control operations. The assumption was that the recruits could apply continuous-processing concepts in the problem-solving R&D plants. That also backfired when the new managers experienced almost complete frustration in their attempt to institute time standards, flexible budgets, and variance reporting in the aerospace environment.

SITUATIONAL DIFFERENCES

In comparing the same positions in different business firms, some similarities and some differences are inevitably found. Purchasing agents, for example, must have a basic knowledge of purchasing principles and methods. However, to assume that those principles and methods can be applied in the same way by a buyer of clothing for a retail store, a buyer of machinery for a construction contractor, and a buyer of transistors for an electronics firm is to ignore completely the situational differences that control the application of the concepts and principles of management. In this example, the differences obviously far exceed the similarities.

All of the preceding examples illustrate the central thesis of this book. To be effective a manager must have two basic areas of understanding: (1) He must understand the operations in his charge and also the principles and concepts of management available to him in handling his supervisory responsibilities. (2) He must also understand the context of the situation that he faces at any particular time. Unless he properly interprets and diagnoses the situation, he cannot determine which concepts or techniques to select in attempting to achieve the results he desires.

The situational void in management theory and practice today has resulted from the effort to accumulate knowledge about management and develop universal principles, techniques, and concepts in practical disregard of situational differences. Writers and researchers have focused on the commonalities among organizations or situations in the hope that they could thereby develop general principles useful for predictive purposes. There has been a definite shortage of comparative studies that attempt to uncover differences and interpret what those differences mean to management theory and practice.

The need for such studies and for a situational model has been recognized for many years. Following World War II American business schools began to teach business policy by the case method. That method is based on the recognition that each firm is unique and that its business policies must reflect that uniqueness. Many of the leading researchers and writers on organization and management theory reached the same conclusions. In 1950 George C. Homans, the sociologist, in his classic *The Human Group,* made the following observations:

> There are no rules for human behavior that apply in every situation without limit or change. . . . In recent years men of practical affairs—industrial executives, for instance—have often come to psychologists and sociologists begging for a plan or set of rules that the executives can apply "across the board"—that is, in all circumstances—in dealing with their employees. There are no such rules, and if there were, they would be dangerous. They might work well for a time; then changing circumstances would make them inappropriate, and the leader would have to deal with a new situation while his mind was clogged with old rules. The maxims of leadership we shall state are, therefore, not to be taken as absolutes but only as convenient guides for the behavior of a leader. They apply only within limits determined by the situation that faces him, and there are situations in which the maxims will conflict with one another. What a leader needs to have is not a set of rules but a good method of analyzing the social situation in which he must act.[1]

In relation to his "good method," Homans says later in his book that "a leader cannot examine the whole situation inside and outside his group unless he has a method for taking up each element of the situation in order and in its relation to the other elements." [2]

Others called for a model to encompass situational differences. Perrow urged that we develop "better classification systems" for dealing with organizations.[3] Fiedler stated that "we require a better method for measuring the favorableness of the leadership situation. . . . We require a scale which is based not only on the presence or absence of good leader-member relations, homogeneity, leader position power, and task structure, but which takes account also of the other factors that are likely to affect the favorableness of the situation." [4] Katz and Kahn proposed that significant dimensions be established for measuring organization structure and function. "Any organization can then be mapped into this set of dimensions and described as being high or low in each." [5]

Many writers and researchers have expressed the need for determining the most effective kinds of leadership or of organization structure, but the broader view relating to all management factors is expressed by John A. Seiler:

> Time and again, managers who are outstandingly successful in one situation perform abysmally in another. Administrators, guided by the good results

of, say, sharing responsibility with a group of subordinates, are frustrated by their failure to replicate those results with another group of associates. What is lacking is a way of making the specifics of each situation reveal the clues upon which appropriate management action can be based. It is not enough to deduce from "currently useful generalizations" what will work. An inductive search for the meaning behind existing behavior is a prerequisite. But the inductive process needs a methodology, some kind of structure which is relevant to any type of organizational setting, yet practical and tangible enough to be put into everyday use.[6]

THE SITUATIONAL MODEL

The situational model presented in this book is intended to fill the need recognized by writers previously cited. Its primary factors are of two types: those internal and those external to the firm. The five primary internal factors are purpose, tasks, technology, people, and structure; the five primary external ones are the political, economic, legal, technical, and social forces and institutions in the firm's environment. But the division of a situation into two sets of factors still provides little information for the manager. He must understand the attributes, composition, current status, and intensity of the factors as well as their interaction if he is to evaluate factor impact when he selects a course of action. For that reason the dimensions of each factor are listed and continuums for the evaluation of the dimensions are supplied.

Advantages of the Model

The situational model presented in this book has eight advantages that can be summarized as follows:

It is a framework that practitioners and others can use to test their experiences. Relating experience to a comprehensive framework provides a better understanding of the forces at work in a situation and the reasons why certain events take place.

It is a convenient framework in which to collect, interrelate, and store management knowledge. The comprehensive nature of the construct makes it useful for classifying, integrating, and testing administrative concepts. Currently our knowledge of management is too loose and unrelated.

It is a model that emphasizes factors and relationships among factors. The focus on interrelationships moves management away from the descriptive emphasis that has often characterized it in the past. Perhaps most important of all, it takes management away from emphasis on a set of rules to the emphasis on a method of analysis. Making comparative studies of organizational factors and viewing the tradeoffs of concepts based on an interpretation of situational variables is a valuable method of analysis that provides considerable insight into management processes.

It depicts dimensions as continuums, which negates the concept of absolutes in management. Different situations are analyzed by comparing the relative status of the significant factors in those situations. The use of standard dimensions measured by scales or continuums should overcome much of the vagueness that typifies management communication and thought.

It serves as a guide for managers in the mapping of situations—one of the ingredients of success in management is the ability to "size up situations." In the long run it should result in improved management action through the more effective application of management concepts and techniques.

It should counter the current tendency to attribute problems to single causes. The model emphasizes the relationship of the many factors in a situation and forces a consideration of the dimensions of those factors. Such an approach to causality is the only sound foundation for the development of a science of management. Situational analysis involves an understanding of management concepts and techniques, the tradeoffs associated with those techniques, and the situational factors that dictate the utilization of specific techniques.

It identifies certain underdeveloped areas of management thought. Management research and writing has tended to concentrate on the structure and people factors. Two of the more important internal factors, tasks and technology, have received far too little attention. The model thus forces a more balanced view of the major factors involved in the management process.

It is useful for dealing with change; it emphasizes the dynamic nature of all the factors in the situation, especially the external ones. It redefines the manager's role as that of successfully adapting the organization to change. Many trends have altered the characteristics of the factors the typical manager faces. Those trends have also resulted in complexity in management that has spurred the search for improved administrative systems and techniques.

It is interesting to note that all of the major forces for change can be accommodated within the situational model. The rapid advance of technology, the increase in the size of business firms, the move to multinational corporations, the information explosion, the increased control of the economy by governments, the involvement of business in social issues, the advance in corporate and personal income, and the public concern with pollution and environmental issues—all are subject to assessment by the dimensions of the factors contained in the situational model.

In summary the situational model of management is directed at overcoming the primary criticism of modern management thought: that it is oversimplified and overgeneralized. As Renate Mayntz says, "propositions which hold for such diverse phenomena as an army, a trade union, and a university must necessarily be either trivial or so abstract as to tell hardly anything of interest about concrete reality." [7] The situational approach is to move management away from those abstractions and generalizations.

LIMITATIONS OF SITUATIONAL ANALYSIS

Situational management theory is obviously not a panacea; there are no miracle solutions to management problems. Just as there are no simple, slick solutions to the crises in cities, pollution, or stock market predictions, so there are no pat answers to how one becomes an effective manager. The complexity of management defies any sort of simplistic remedies. What is needed is a feel for the theoretical direction in which management thought must move, and not another attractive fad.

The situational approach has three primary limitations as a method for evaluating management processes. The first is its complexity. Even relatively simple situations are composed of a number of factors, each of which has several dimensions. Models are of value because they simplify the real world; but if the model itself is complex, its usefulness is reduced. As is true of any other model, experience in working with it results in its becoming more automatic and natural; but if care is not taken in its use, it can entangle situations rather than unravel them. However, one of the real values of the situational model is that it forces the user to face up to the complexity of management. By being compelled to consider a broad range of variables, the manager is made aware of the institutions, forces, processes, and elements that have a bearing on his decision making.

In evaluating a situation, a manager should consider the factors that account for most of its conditions. It might be said arbitrarily that if he accounts for 80 percent of the factors, he will probably make decisions that would not have been significantly different if he had accounted for all of them. That is, the effort of uncovering the other 20 percent might not be worthwhile, especially if the model is thereby so complicated that it becomes confusing.

The second limitation is the difficulty of considering all situations to fit one generalized model. Many critics feel that situations have so many unique characteristics that it is impossible to include all their factors in one construct. They argue that we cannot cram all managerial experience into one model and that, even if we could, we cannot accurately assess it.

Questions such as the following are asked: How do you accurately measure the intensity of factors? How do you weight the various factors? Is the scale for each dimension really linear, or is it curvilinear or even discontinuous? Can anyone really identify cause-and-effect relationships?

Admittedly the model structure is developmental and needs considerable refinement. However, at this stage the details of the model are less important than the general relationships. If the relationships are valid and if the methodology is useful, experience and research will take care of the details. Also, directing management thought away from descriptive, single-cause approaches toward relationships-oriented, systems methodology is a step toward advancing our understanding of the basic nature of management. Management thought has developed slowly because of the complicated nature of human relations. Expansion of our understanding of management is therefore dependent on dealing with that complexity.

A third limitation of the model is a weakness commonly found in planning and control systems: Most systems and models concentrate on activities or events that are easily measured and tend to ignore those that are not. When physical dimensions can be measured or objects can be counted, the control systems tend to concentrate on physical attributes. The situational model too has a large number of dimensions of physical tasks and organization structure, but fewer of such abstractions as psychological attributes, informal structure, and environmental forces. There is an obvious imbalance in the model, but the same imbalance is found in our knowledge about management. That imbalance should eventually be corrected as accuracy is gained in assessing technology, understanding human behavior, and dealing with the other more nebulous components of a firm's environment.

IMPROVEMENTS NEEDED IN THE MODEL

Many of the improvements needed in the model are obvious: More dimensions should be added to increase relevance; the continuum concept needs clarification and standardization; more understanding of cause-and-effect relationships and dependency considerations is needed; and research and experimentation must be broadened to determine the validity and reliability of the overall model and the individual dimensions.

One of the important advances necessary to enhance the value of the model lies in a slightly different realm. If the model becomes so standardized that it can be used to evaluate a broad range of situations, profiles of those situations can be drawn and will then be useful for comparative and analytical purposes. Given a common set of variables and dimensions that are subject to specific identification through the use of scales or continuums, profiles or graphs of the characteristics of situations are possible.

The situational profiles would be much like the personality profiles currently in use to represent the traits or abilities of individuals graphically. There is no reason why the same methodology cannot be used for tasks, organization structure, people, technology, or any other factor in the situational model. In a more complex way it could be done for the entire model or situation. Such profiles could open new avenues for research and analysis of management functions. They could provide the data necessary to classify, compare, and evaluate different situations. Probably no greater stimulus could be given to the advance of manage-

Figure 11. Situation profiles of an R&D and a production organization.

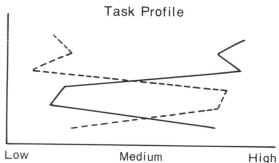

Repetition
Specialization
Sequential interdependence
Time range
Autonomy
Throughput rate

Task Profile

Low   Medium   High

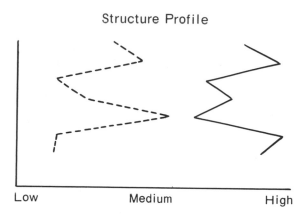

Scale
Hierarchy
Centralization
Span of control
Integration
Formalization
Job specifications

Structure Profile

Low   Medium   High

——————— Production organization
----------- R&D organization

177

ment theory and practice than by a valid way to classify and compare situational differences.

Figure 11 is an example of the profiles that could be developed; it presents two factors for an R&D and a production firm, both hypothetical. The top graph includes some of the crucial dimensions of the task factor. Production tasks are highly repetitive, narrowly specialized, and sequentially interrelated with a short job cycle; they permit little autonomy, and they are large in volume. Research and development tasks are characterized by almost the opposite features, and that is immediately apparent in the upper half of Figure 11.

The lower half of Figure 11 is the structure profile of the same R&D and production operations. The R&D laboratory is small in size, has few levels in the hierarchy, is decentralized, and has a low span of control. The tasks are moderately integrated, and there is little formalization of structure or job specifications. The production plant is much larger in size, has many levels in its chain of command, is more centralized, and has a broader span of control. Structural integration is moderate, and both structure and job specifications are much more formalized. Again the profiles accurately represent the differences between the two. Capitalizing on the potential value of the situational approach to management is linked to the development of an easier way to work with the construct. The profile approach appears to offer this methodology.

Status of Situational Analysis Approach

Management thought is still in the early stages of its evolution; in its brief history it has not advanced beyond the preliminary formulations of its theoretical structure. However, it is at a point of maturity where the principles or universal process approach must be superseded by a framework that will provide a breakthrough in advancing to a higher stage of knowledge. Situational analysis offers a relationships-oriented approach that is better suited to the actual complexity of management. It is true that situational approach itself is in the early stages of development, so that it also suffers from lack of maturity, but even these crude beginnings point the new direction in which management theory and practice appear to be evolving.

references

CHAPTER 1

1. Henri Fayol, *General and Industrial Management* (London: Sir Isaac Pitman & Sons, Ltd., 1949), p. 42.
2. Ibid., p. 19.

CHAPTER 4

1. Alain C. Enthoven and K. Wayne Smith, *How Much Is Enough?* (New York: Harper & Row, Publishers, Incorporated, 1971), p. 6.
2. John J. Morse and Jay W. Lorsch, "Beyond Theory Y," *Harvard Business Review,* May–June 1970, p. 68.

CHAPTER 5

1. Richard Johnson, Fremont E. Kast, and James E. Rosenzweig, *The Theory and Management of Systems* (New York: McGraw-Hill Book Company, 1963), p. 4.
2. R. L. Ackoff, "Systems, Organizations, and Interdisciplinary Research," in F. E. Emery (Ed.), *Systems Thinking* (Middlesex, England: Penguin Books Ltd., 1969), p. 332.
3. Kenneth Boulding, "General Systems Theory—The Skeleton of Science," *Management Science,* April 1956, pp. 197–208.
4. Thomas A. Petit, "A Behavioral Theory of Management," *Academy of Management Journal,* December 1967, pp. 341–350.

CHAPTER 6

1. Eliot D. Chapple and Leonard R. Sayles, *The Measure of Management* (New York: Macmillan Publishing Co., Inc., 1961), p. 44.
2. Joan Woodward, *Industrial Organization: Theory and Practice* (London: Oxford University Press, 1965), p. 51.
3. Arthur H. Walker and Jay W. Lorsch, "Organizational Choice: Product Versus Function," in Jay W. Lorsch and Paul R. Lawrence (Eds.), *Studies in Organization Design* (Homewood, Ill.: Richard D. Irwin, Inc., 1970), p. 51.
4. Charles Perrow, "A Framework for the Comparative Analysis of Organizations," *American Sociological Review,* Vol. 32, No. 2, 1967, p. 195.
5. Chapple and Sayles, op. cit., p. 100.
6. Fred Fiedler, *A Theory of Leadership Effectiveness* (New York: McGraw-Hill Book Company, 1967), p. 246.
7. *Dictionary of Occupational Titles* (Washington, D.C.: U.S. Government Printing Office, 1965).

8. Jerald Hage and Michael Aiken, "Routine Technology, Social Structure, and Organizational Goals," *Administrative Science Quarterly,* September 1969, pp. 366–376.
9. James R. Bright, *Research, Development, and Technological Innovation* (Homewood, Ill.: Richard D. Irwin, Inc., 1964), p. vi.
10. Stanley H. Udy, Jr., "The Comparative Analysis of Organizations," in James G. March (Ed.), *Handbook of Organizations* (Chicago: Rand McNally & Company, 1965), p. 701.
11. Warren G. Bennis, *Changing Organizations* (New York: McGraw-Hill Book Company, 1966), p. 12.
12. Paul R. Lawrence and Jay W. Lorsch, *Organization and Environment* (Homewood, Ill.: Richard D. Irwin, Inc., 1969), p. 182.

CHAPTER 7

1. Stanley H. Udy, Jr., The Comparative Analysis of Organizations," in James G. March (Ed.), *Handbook of Organizations* (Chicago: Rand McNally & Company, 1965), p. 693.
2. John J. Morse and Jay W. Lorsch, "Beyond Theory Y," *Harvard Business Review,* May–June 1970, pp. 61–68.
3. Ibid., p. 68.
4. Ernest Dale, "Some Foundations of Organization Theory," *California Management Review,* Fall 1959, p. 84.

CHAPTER 8

1. Alain C. Enthoven and K. Wayne Smith, *How Much Is Enough?* (New York: Harper & Row, Publishers, Incorporated, 1971), p. 105.
2. *Social Responsibilities of Business Corporations* (New York: Committee for Economic Development, 1971), p. 59. A Statement by the Research and Policy Committee.
3. Daniel Katz and Robert L. Kahn, *The Social Psychology of Organizations* (New York: John Wiley & Sons, Inc., 1966), p. 268.

CHAPTER 9

1. Fred Fiedler, *A Theory of Leadership Effectiveness* (New York: McGraw-Hill Book Company, 1967), p. 261.
2. Ibid., p. 262.
3. Rensis Likert, *New Patterns of Management* (New York: McGraw-Hill Book Company, Inc., 1961), pp. 94–95.
4. Paul R. Lawrence and Jay W. Lorsch, *Organization and Environment* (Homewood, Ill.: Richard D. Irwin, Inc., 1969), p. 183.
5. J. Sterling Livingston, "Myth of the Well-Educated Manager," *Harvard Business Review,* January–February 1971, p. 87.

CHAPTER 10

1. David C. McClelland, "Business Drive and National Achievement," *Harvard Business Review,* July–August 1962, p. 112.

CHAPTER 12

1. George C. Homans, *The Human Group* (New York: Harcourt, Brace and Company, Inc., 1950), p. 424.
2. Ibid., p. 435.
3. Charles Perrow, "A Framework for the Comparative Analysis of Organizations," *American Sociological Review*, Vol. 32, No. 2, 1967, p. 205.
4. Fred Fiedler, *A Theory of Leadership Effectiveness* (New York: McGraw-Hill Book Company, 1967), p. 262.
5. Daniel Katz and Robert L. Kahn, *The Social Psychology of Organizations* (New York: John Wiley & Sons, Inc., 1966), p. 111.
6. John A. Seiler, *Systems Analysis in Organizational Behavior* (Homewood, Ill.: Richard D. Irwin, Inc., 1967), p. x.
7. Renate Mayntz, "The Study of Organizations: A Trend Report and Bibliography," *Current Sociology*, Vol. XIII, No. 3, p. 113.

index